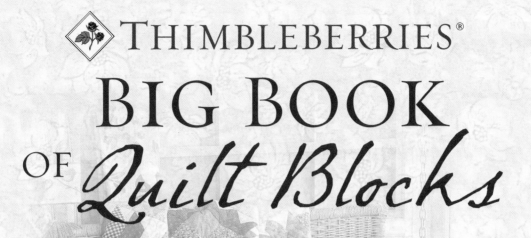

THIMBLEBERRIES®
BIG BOOK
OF *Quilt Blocks*

LYNETTE JENSEN

Knapp
K
P
Press

Copyright© 2005 by Publishing Solutions, LLC.

Projects Copyright© 2005 by Lynette Jensen.

This book was designed, produced and published by Knapp Press, an imprint of Publishing Solutions, LLC.
1107 Hazeltine Boulevard
Chaska, MN 55318

President – James L. Knapp
Creative Director – Lynette Jensen
Photostyling – Carole Brueggeman, Tom Henry, Dan Thornberg
Additional Photograph, page 3 – Marilyn Ginsburg
Technical Writer – Sue Bahr
Technical Illustrator – Lisa Kirchoff
Assistant Technical Illustrator – Megan Lueneburg
Project Management – Jim Bindas/Book Productions LLC
Proofreader – Janice Cauley

Cover and interior design by Koechel Peterson & Associates, Inc., Minneapolis, Minnesota

We wish to thank the support staff of THIMBLEBERRIES® Design Studio: Sherry Husske, Virginia Brodd, Renae Ashwill, Ardelle Paulson, Kathy Lobeck, and Julie Jergens.

Our Promise to You: All projects in this book have been created in their entirety by the staff at THIMBLEBERRIES Design Studio. The accuracy of our patterns and instructions has been thoroughly tested.

10 9 8 7 6 5 4
Library of Congress Control Number: 2005927049
Printed in the United States of America.

ISBN: 1-932533-05-2
13-Digit ISBN: 978-1-932533-05-7

Table of Contents

ACKNOWLEDGMENTS

*T*he world of quilting and quilt design has been a very important part of my life for a very long time. I have always been very grateful for all that I have learned from my grandmother and my parents that led me to this wonderful craft. Through THIMBLEBERRIES, I have created a common bond with quilters around the world who also embrace this wonderful heritage craft and use it to decorate their homes and enrich the lives of friends and family.

THIMBLEBERRIES is more than just me and I would like to thank all of the THIMBLEBERRIES team for their work in putting this book together, especially Sue Bahr, Lisa Kirchoff, and Megan Leuneburg for their technical skills in the creation of this book. They are all a joy to work with and I am blessed to have them in my life.

FOREWORD

*S*everal years ago, recognizing the limited time many quilters have to devote to their craft, I started THIMBLEBERRIES Block-of-the-Month. The concept was simple: provide quilters a quilt block to do each month and, by the end of the year, the 12 individual blocks could be pieced into a single, beautiful quilt.

Beginning with the series THIMBLEBERRIES MONTH BY MONTH, the concept was overwhelmingly embraced by many of the approximately 2500 quilt shops that carry THIMBLEBERRIES fabric and by the quilters they serve. Beginning in 1998 and continuing in subsequent years, the concept was expanded with THIMBLEBERRIES VILLAGE™, SAFE HAVEN™, A QUILTER'S GARDEN™, and PANSY PARK™.

Through the years, the basic premise has remained the same: quilt one block at a time until all the blocks for a glorious quilt are made. By combining this block-a-month approach with the distinctive THIMBLEBERRIES coordination of colors, prints and patterns, we have created a winning formula for beginner and experienced quilters alike.

In this book, you will find 60 different quilt blocks that combine to make five specific quilts. However, the beauty of blocks is that they can be enjoyed either individually or in combination to make smaller projects—wall hangings, pillows, table toppers and table runners. Let your imagination be your guide in this book and you will not be disappointed.

Sincerely,

Lynette Jensen

INTRODUCTION

❧

A home is never more comfortable and beautiful than when it is graced by a quilt. The colors, designs, fabrics and the thousands of stitches that comprise a quilt suggest a depth of feeling that is welcoming and comforting to you, your family and guests. Decorating your home with quilts will convey a feeling of well-being that comes from being surrounded by the colors, textures and patterns that reflect your personal taste.

If you value a hand-crafted approach to accessorizing your home, this book is for you. For over 16 years, THIMBLEBERRIES has been dedicated to providing quilting inspirations that combine a love of color and design. This book provides both beginners and experienced quilters with 60 wonderful quilt blocks that celebrate both color and design.

These blocks can be stand-alone projects, pieced into one of five wonderful quilts included here, or they can launch you into a number of different creative paths. A quilt block is the beginning point of any quilt. Piece one block and you are on your way. A block can be repeated in a quilt, or it can be combined with other blocks to create a different design.

We have broken quiltmaking into its most basic activities. By making one block at a time, you learn the quilt craft the way it has been practiced for hundreds of years. The blocks have

been chosen for their straightforward and uncomplicated design as well as their beauty and long-lasting appeal.

This book offers a mixture of techniques for various skill levels. It is progressive in its approach in that the blocks and quilts at the beginning of the book are less complicated than those at the end. You will learn quilt-making basics as you progress through this book. There is a broad range of quilt designs in this book, from casual to formal. Each quilt also represents a different quilt-making style.

Our emphasis has always been on beauty and simplicity. The selected quilts have a strong, traditional approach. Your time commitment will be kept to a minimum without requiring expensive or hard-to-find tools. And your quilt will stand the test of time and become a family heirloom.

The THIMBLEBERRIES approach is to build confidence in your ability to surround yourself with easily coordinated furnishings while suggesting a cozy and comfortable lifestyle. And your quilts will work in either a traditional or contemporary home.

Although these 60 blocks combine to make five specific quilts, you are encouraged to be creative. For example, small quilts made from single blocks can produce very big decorative results. Don't overlook the numerous opportunities throughout your home to showcase small quilts.

The blocks in this book feature attention to detail and easy-to-follow, illustrated instructions, and have a traditional appeal and will help you achieve a warm, classic, country feeling in your decorating.

MONTH *by* MONTH

Meaningful times and seasons come alive in this quilt that reflects the fabric of our lives.

THIMBLEBERRIES MONTH BY MONTH was the beginning of the THIMBLEBERRIES Block-of-the-Month series. The concept was simple: piece one block a month and, at the end of the year, piece the 12 blocks together for a stunning, beautiful quilt. I wanted the ease of MONTH BY MONTH to be readily apparent to anyone who sees this quilt. By focusing on making only one block every month, we removed the intimidating time commitment required for making a full-size, 62-inch by 78-inch quilt.

Quilters responded enthusiastically to THIMBLEBERRIES MONTH BY MONTH. Each block represents its month in an understated, classically country manner. Whether it's the hearts of February, the tulips of April, July's red-white-and-blue celebration or December's Christmas tree, this quilt represented a celebration of the whole year.

The quilt blocks in MONTH BY MONTH are separated by lattice pieces with the blocks running row by row in a traditional quilt setting. While making this quilt, you will be developing and improving your quilting skills. Please refer to page 244 for complete quilting instructions.

As with all THIMBLEBERRIES quilts, pay special attention to the use and integration of color in the blocks and the quilt.

15

MONTH
by MONTH

62 x 78 inches

Fabrics & Supplies

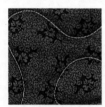

1-1/2 yards
BEIGE PRINT
for all 12 blocks

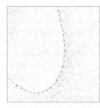

3/8 yard
MEDIUM BLUE PRINT
for blocks 1, 6
1/4 yard for block borders

1/3 yard
RED PRINT #1
for blocks 2, 3, 7
1/4 yard for block borders

1/3 yard
RED PRINT #2
for blocks 2, 4, 5
1/4 yard for block borders

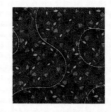

1/3 yard
RED PRINT #3
for blocks 2, 9, 12
1/4 yard for block borders

1/4 yard
GREEN PRINT #1
for blocks 2, 4, 8, 10, 11
1/4 yard for block borders

1/2 yard
GREEN PRINT #2
for blocks 3, 4, 9, 10, 12
1/4 yard for block borders

5" x 18" piece
GREEN CHECK
for block 3
1/4 yard for block borders

1/3 yard
DARK BLUE PRINT
for blocks 4, 7
1/4 yard for block borders

1/4 yard
LIGHT GOLD PRINT
for blocks 4, 11
1/4 yard for block borders

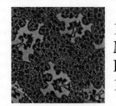

1/4 yard
MEDIUM BROWN PRINT for blocks 8, 11
1/4 yard for block borders

1/8 yard
GREEN PRINT #3
for blocks 4, 9
1/4 yard for block borders

7" x 20" piece
DARK BROWN PRINT
for blocks 8, 9
1/4 yard for block borders

1/4 yard
BLUE FLORAL
for block 5
1/4 yard for block borders

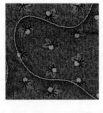

7" x 8" piece
ORANGE PRINT #1
for block 10
1/4 yard for block borders

1/3 yard
GOLD PRINT #1
for blocks 6, 8, 9
1/4 yard for block borders

7" x 8" piece
ORANGE PRINT #2
for block 10
1/4 yard for block borders

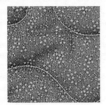

1/4 yard
GOLD PRINT #2
for block 7
1/4 yard for block borders

7" x 8" piece
ORANGE PRINT #3
for block 10
1/4 yard for block borders

3/8 yard
GOLD PRINT #3
for inner border

1-1/2 yards
GREEN/RUST FLORAL
for outer border

2/3 yard
GREEN PRINT #2
for binding

4-2/3 yards backing fabric
quilt batting, at least
66 x 82-inches

Before beginning this project, read through **Getting Started** on page 244.

*This fabric key should be used as a helpful guideline in selecting fabric for your quilt project.
We cannot guarantee that a specific fabric will be available at your favorite quilt store,
but suitable substitutions can be found.*

MONTH *by* MONTH
BLOCK I - *January*

CUTTING

From MEDIUM BLUE PRINT:

❋ Cut 1, 4-1/2 x 42-inch strip.
   From the strip cut:
   1, 4-1/2-inch square
   8, 2-1/2-inch squares
❋ Cut 1, 2-1/2 x 42-inch strip.
   From the strip cut:
   8, 2-1/2 x 4-1/2-inch rectangles

From BEIGE PRINT:

❋ Cut 2, 2-1/2 x 42-inch strips.
   From the strips cut:
   24, 2-1/2-inch squares

PIECING

Step 1 ❧ Sew the 2-1/2-inch **MEDIUM BLUE** squares and 8 of the 2-1/2-inch **BEIGE** squares together in pairs; press. Sew the pairs together; press.

Make 8   Make 4

Step 2 ❧ With right sides together, position a 2-1/2-inch **BEIGE** square on the corner of a 2-1/2 x 4-1/2-inch **MEDIUM BLUE** rectangle. Draw a diagonal line on the square and stitch on the line. Trim the seam allowance to 1/4-inch; press. Repeat this process at the opposite corner of the rectangle.

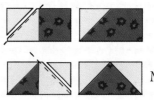

Make 8

Step 3 ❧ Sew the Step 2 units together in pairs; press.

Make 4

20

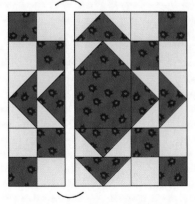

MONTH BY MONTH Block 1

Step 4 ✐ Sew Step 3 units to the top and bottom edges of the 4-1/2-inch **MEDIUM BLUE** square; press. Sew the Step 1 units to both side edges of the remaining Step 3 units; press. Sew the units to the side edges of the block; press. *At this point the block should measure 12-1/2-inches square.*

MONTH *by* MONTH
BLOCK 2 - *February*

CUTTING

From the RED PRINTS #1, #2, and #3:
❊ Cut 1, 4-1/2 x 6-1/2-inch rectangle from each fabric
❊ Cut 1, 2-1/2 x 4-1/2-inch rectangle from each fabric

From GREEN PRINT #1:
❊ Cut 4, 2-1/2-inch squares

From BEIGE PRINT:
❊ Cut 1, 2-1/2 x 42-inch strip.
   From the strip cut:
      8, 2-1/2-inch squares
      12, 1-1/2-inch squares

PIECING

Step 1 ✒ With right sides together, position 1-1/2-inch **BEIGE** squares on the upper corners of the 2-1/2 x 4-1/2-inch **RED #1** rectangle. Draw a diagonal line on the squares; stitch, trim, and press. Repeat this process for the 2-1/2 x 4-1/2-inch **RED #2** and **RED #3** rectangles. Sew a 2-1/2-inch **BEIGE** square to the right edge of each of the units; press.

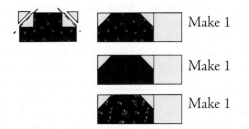

Make 1

Make 1

Make 1

Step 2 ✒ With right sides together, position 1-1/2-inch **BEIGE** squares on the upper corners of the 4-1/2 x 6-1/2-inch **RED #1** rectangle. Draw a diagonal line on the squares; stitch, trim, and press. Repeat this process for the 4-1/2 x 6-1/2-inch **RED #2** and **RED #3** rectangles. Sew the corresponding Step 1 units to the left edge of each of these units; press. *At this point each heart square should measure 6-1/2-inches square.*
(*see diagram on following page*)

22

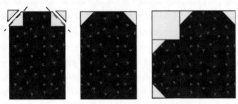

Make 1 heart square from
Red #1, **Red #2**, and **Red #3**

Step 3 ✒ Sew 2-1/2-inch **BEIGE** squares to both side edges of 2 of the 2-1/2-inch **GREEN #1** squares; press. Sew 2-1/2-inch **GREEN #1** squares to both side edges of a 2-1/2-inch **BEIGE** square; press. Sew the units together; press. *At this point the nine-patch square should measure 6-1/2-inches square.*

Make 1 nine-patch square

Step 4 ✒ Sew the nine-patch square to the right edge of the **RED #1** heart square; press.

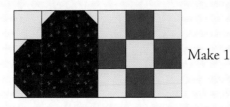

Make 1

Step 5 ✒ Sew the **RED #2** and **RED #3** heart squares together; press.

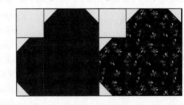

Make 1

Step 6 ✒ Sew the Step 4 unit to the top edge of the Step 5 unit; press. *At this point the block should measure 12-1/2-inches square.*

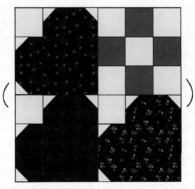

MONTH BY MONTH Block 2

MONTH *by* MONTH
BLOCK 3 - *March*

CUTTING

From RED PRINT #1:
❋ Cut 1, 4-1/2-inch square
❋ Cut 4, 2-1/2-inch squares

From GREEN PRINT #2:
❋ Cut 1, 2-1/2 x 42-inch strip.
   From the strip cut:
      4, 2-1/2-inch squares
      4, 2-1/2 x 4-1/2-inch rectangles

From GREEN CHECK:
❋ Cut 4, 2-7/8-inch squares

From BEIGE PRINT:
❋ Cut 4, 2-7/8-inch squares
❋ Cut 1, 2-1/2 x 42-inch strip.
   From the strip cut:
      8, 2-1/2-inch squares
      4, 2-1/2 x 4-1/2-inch rectangles

PIECING

Step 1 ✌ With right sides together, layer the 2-7/8-inch **GREEN CHECK** and **BEIGE** squares together in pairs. Cut the layered squares in half diagonally to make 8 sets of triangles. Stitch 1/4-inch from the diagonal edge of each pair of triangles to make 8 triangle-pieced squares; press.

Make 8, 2-1/2-inch triangle-pieced squares

Step 2 ✌ Sew the 2-1/2-inch **RED #1** squares to 4 of the triangle-pieced squares; press. Sew the 2-1/2-inch **GREEN #2** squares to 4 of the triangle-pieced squares; press. Sew the units together in pairs; press.

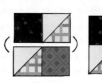

Make 4

Step 3 ✒ With right sides together, position a 2-1/2-inch **BEIGE** square on the corner of a 2-1/2 x 4-1/2-inch **GREEN #2** rectangle. Draw a diagonal line on the square; stitch, trim, and press. Repeat this process at the opposite corner of the rectangles.

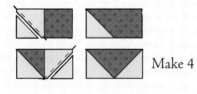

Make 4

Step 4 ✒ Sew 2-1/2 x 4-1/2-inch **BEIGE** rectangles to the bottom edge of the Step 3 units; press.

Make 4

Step 5 ✒ Sew the Step 2 units to both side edges of 2 of the Step 4 units; press.

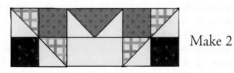

Make 2

Step 6 ✒ Sew 2 of the Step 4 units to the top and bottom edges of the 4-1/2-inch **RED #1** square; press. Sew the Step 5 units to the side edges of the block; press. *At this point the block should measure 12-1/2-inches square.*

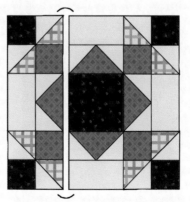

MONTH BY MONTH Block 3

MONTH *by* MONTH
BLOCK 4 - *April*

CUTTING

From the DARK BLUE PRINT, LIGHT GOLD PRINT, and RED PRINT #2:
❊ Cut 1, 5-1/4-inch square from each fabric. Cut the squares diagonally into quarters. You will be using only 1 triangle from each fabric.
❊ Cut 1, 4-7/8-inch square from each fabric. Cut the squares in half diagonally. You will be using only 1 triangle from each fabric.

From GREEN PRINT #3:
❊ Cut 1, 2 x 42-inch strip.
  From the strip cut:
    1, 2 x 8-1/2-inch rectangle
    1, 2 x 6-1/2-inch rectangle
    2, 2 x 4-1/2-inch rectangles

From GREEN PRINT #1:
❊ Cut 1, 2 x 18-inch strip.
  From the strip cut:
    1, 2 x 8-1/2-inch rectangle
    1, 2 x 6-1/2-inch rectangle

From GREEN PRINT #2:
❊ Cut 1, 1-1/2 x 42-inch strip.
  From the strip cut:
    2, 1-1/2 x 8-1/2-inch rectangles
    1, 1-1/2 x 4-1/2-inch rectangle

From BEIGE PRINT:
❊ Cut 1, 5-1/4 x 42-inch strip.
  From the strip cut:
    1, 5-1/4-inch square. Cut the square diagonally into quarters. You will be using only 3 of the triangles.
    1, 4-1/2-inch square
    2, 2 x 4-inch rectangles
    4, 2-inch squares

Piecing

Step 1 ✂ Sew the **BEIGE** triangles to each of the **DARK BLUE, LIGHT GOLD,** and **RED #2** triangles; press. Sew a corresponding color triangle to each of these units; press.

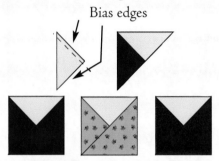

Bias edges

Make 1 flower from each fabric

Step 2 ✂ With right sides together, position a 2 x 4-inch **BEIGE** rectangle on the corner of the 2 x 6-1/2-inch **GREEN #3** rectangle. Draw a diagonal line on the **BEIGE** rectangle; stitch, trim, and press. Repeat this process for the 2 x 6-1/2-inch **GREEN #1** rectangle, notice the placement of the 2 x 4-inch **BEIGE** rectangle and direction of the stitching line. Sew the 2 leaf units to both side edges of a 1-1/2 x 8-1/2-inch **GREEN #2** rectangle; press. Sew the **DARK BLUE** flower unit to the top edge of this unit; press.

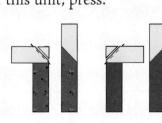

Make 1

Step 3 ✂ With right sides together, position a 2-inch **BEIGE** square on the corner of a 2 x 4-1/2-inch **GREEN #3** rectangle. Draw a diagonal line on the square; stitch, trim, and press. Repeat this process for the remaining 2 x 4-1/2-inch **GREEN #3** rectangle, notice the direction of the stitching line. Sew the 2 leaf units to both side edges of the 1-1/2 x 4-1/2-inch **GREEN #2** rectangle; press. Sew the **LIGHT GOLD** flower unit and the 4-1/2-inch **BEIGE** square to the top edge of this unit; press.

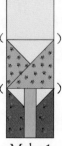

(continued on the next page)

Make 1

27

Step 4 ✌ With right sides together, position a 2-inch **BEIGE** square on the corner of the 2 x 8-1/2-inch **GREEN #1** rectangle. Draw a diagonal line on the square; stitch, trim, and press. Repeat this process for the 2 x 8-1/2-inch **GREEN #3** rectangle, notice the direction of the stitching line. Sew the 2 leaf units to both side edges of a 1-1/2 x 8-1/2-inch **GREEN #2** rectangle; press. Sew the **RED #2** flower unit to the top edge of this unit; press.

Step 5 ✌ Sew together the units from Step 2, Step 3, and Step 4; press. *At this point the block should measure 12-1/2-inches square.*

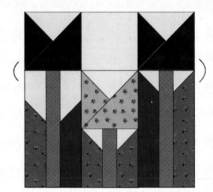

MONTH BY MONTH BLOCK 4

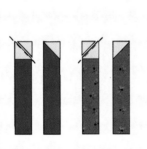

Make 1

MONTH *by* MONTH
BLOCK 5 - *May*

CUTTING

From BLUE FLORAL:
❊ Cut 1, 6-7/8 x 42-inch strip.
From the strip cut:
    1, 6-7/8-inch square
    5, 2-1/2 x 4-1/2-inch rectangles

From RED PRINT #2:
❊ Cut 1, 2-1/2 x 42-inch strip.
From this strip cut:
    12, 2-1/2-inch squares

From BEIGE PRINT:
❊ Cut 1, 6-7/8 x 42-inch strip.
From the strip cut:
    1, 6-7/8-inch square
    2, 4-1/2-inch squares
    4, 2-1/2 x 4-1/2-inch rectangles
    2, 2-1/2-inch squares

PIECING

Step 1 ✍ With right sides together, layer the 6-7/8-inch **BLUE FLORAL** and **BEIGE** squares. Cut the layered square in half diagonally. Stitch 1/4-inch from the diagonal edge of each pair of triangles; press. *At this point each triangle-pieced square should measure 6-1/2-inches square.*

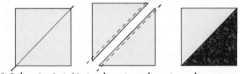

Make 2, 6-1/2-inch triangle-pieced squares

Step 2 ✍ With right sides together, position a 4-1/2-inch **BEIGE** square on the **BLUE FLORAL** corner of the triangle-pieced squares. Draw a diagonal line on the **BEIGE** squares; stitch, trim, and press. Sew the units together; press. *At this point the unit should measure 6-1/2 x 12-1/2-inches.*

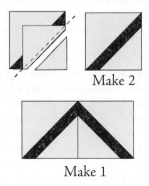

Make 2

Make 1

Step 3 ✍ With right sides together, position a 2-1/2-inch **RED #2** square on the corner of a 2-1/2 x 4-1/2-inch **BLUE FLORAL** rectangle. Draw a diagonal line on the square; stitch, trim, and press. Repeat this process at the opposite corner of the rectangle.

Make 3

Step 4 ✍ With right sides together, position a 2-1/2-inch **BEIGE** square on the left corner of a 2-1/2 x 4-1/2-inch **BLUE FLORAL** rectangle. Draw a diagonal line on the square; stitch, trim, and press. Position a 2-1/2-inch **RED #2** square on the opposite corner of the rectangle. Draw a diagonal line on the square; stitch, trim, and press.

Make 1

Step 5 ✍ With right sides together, position a 2-1/2-inch **RED #2** square on the left corner of a 2-1/2 x 4-1/2-inch **BLUE FLORAL** rectangle. Draw a diagonal line on the square; stitch, trim, and press. Position a 2-1/2-inch **BEIGE** square on the opposite corner of the rectangle. Draw a diagonal line on the square; stitch, trim, and press.

Make 1

Step 6 ✍ Sew the Step 4 unit to the left edge of a Step 3 unit. Sew the Step 5 unit to the right edge of this unit; press. *At this point the unit should measure 2-1/2 x 12-1/2-inches.*

Make 1

(continued on the next page)

Step 7 ✒ With right sides together, position a 2-1/2-inch **RED #2** square on the left corner of a 2-1/2 x 4-1/2-inch **BEIGE** rectangle. Draw a diagonal line on the **RED #2** square; stitch, trim, and press. Make 2 units. Repeat this process positioning a 2-1/2-inch **RED #2** square on the right corner of a 2-1/2 x 4-1/2-inch **BEIGE** rectangle. Make 2 units.

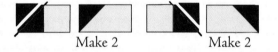

Make 2   Make 2

Step 8 ✒ Referring to the diagram, sew the Step 7 units to both side edges of the Step 3 units; press. Make 2 units and sew them together; press. *At this point the unit should measure 4-1/2 x 12-1/2-inches.*

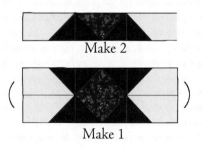

Make 2

Make 1

Step 9 ✒ Sew together the units from Step 2, Step 6, and Step 8; press. *At this point the unit should measure 12-1/2-inches square.*

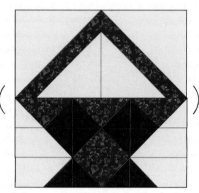

MONTH BY MONTH Block 5

MONTH *by* MONTH
BLOCK 6 - *June*

CUTTING

From MEDIUM BLUE PRINT:
❊ Cut 1, 4-1/2 x 42-inch strip.
   From the strip cut:
      1, 4-1/2-inch square
      4, 2-1/2-inch squares
      4, 2-1/2 x 4-1/2-inch rectangles

From GOLD PRINT #1:
❊ Cut 2, 2-7/8-inch squares
❊ Cut 1, 2-1/2 x 42-inch strip.
   From the strip cut:
      4, 2-1/2-inch squares
      4, 2-1/2 x 6-1/2-inch rectangles

From BEIGE PRINT:
❊ Cut 1, 2-7/8 x 42-inch strip.
   From the strip cut:
      2, 2-7/8-inch squares
      8, 2-1/2-inch squares
      2, 2-1/2 x 4-1/2-inch rectangles

PIECING

Step 1 ✍ With right sides together, layer the 2-7/8-inch **GOLD #1** and **BEIGE** squares together in pairs. Cut the layered squares in half diagonally to make 4 sets of triangles. Stitch 1/4-inch from the diagonal edge of each set of triangles; press.

Make 4, 2-1/2-inch triangle-pieced squares

Step 2 ✍ With right sides together, position 2-1/2-inch **BEIGE** squares on the corners of a 2-1/2 x 6-1/2-inch **GOLD #1** rectangle. Draw a diagonal line on the squares; stitch, trim, and press. Sew the units together in pairs; press.

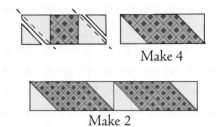

Make 4

Make 2

Step 3 ✷ With right sides together, position a 2-1/2-inch **GOLD #1** square on the corner of a 2-1/2 x 4-1/2-inch **BEIGE** rectangle. Draw a diagonal line on the square; stitch, trim, and press. Repeat this process at the opposite corner of the rectangle.

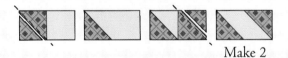

Make 2

Step 4 ✷ Sew together 2 of the 2-1/2-inch **MEDIUM BLUE** squares, 1 of the 2-1/2 x 4-1/2-inch **MEDIUM BLUE** rectangles, and 2 of the triangle-pieced squares; press.

Make 2

Step 5 ✷ Sew together 2 of the 2-1/2 x 4-1/2-inch **MEDIUM BLUE** rectangles, the 4-1/2-inch **MEDIUM BLUE** square, and 2 units from Step 3; press.

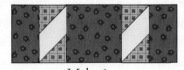

Make 1

Step 6 ✷ Sew together the units from Step 2, Step 4, and Step 5; press. *At this point the block should measure 12-1/2-inches square.*

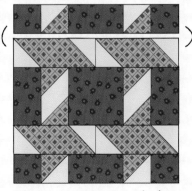

35

MONTH *by* MONTH
BLOCK 7 - *July*

CUTTING

From GOLD PRINT #2:
❋ Cut 1, 4-1/2 x 42-inch strip.
  From the strip cut:
    1, 4-1/2-inch square
    8, 2-1/2-inch squares

From DARK BLUE PRINT:
❋ Cut 1, 2-1/2 x 42-inch strip.
  From the strip cut:
    8, 2-1/2-inch squares
    4, 2-1/2 x 4-1/2-inch rectangles

From RED PRINT #1:
❋ Cut 1, 2-1/2 x 42-inch strip.
  From the strip cut:
    3, 2-1/2 x 13-inch strips

From BEIGE PRINT:
❋ Cut 1, 1-1/2 x 42-inch strip.
  From the strip cut:
    2, 1-1/2 x 13-inch strips

PIECING

Step 1 ✒ With right sides together, position a 2-1/2-inch **GOLD #2** square on the corner of a 2-1/2 x 4-1/2-inch **DARK BLUE** rectangle. Draw a diagonal line on the square; stitch, trim, and press. Repeat this process at the opposite corner of the rectangle.

Make 4 Star
Point Units

Step 2 ✒ Sew 2-1/2-inch **DARK BLUE** squares to both sides edges of 2 of the Step 1 star point units; press.

Make 2

Step 3 ✒ Sew 2 star point units to the top and bottom edges of the 4-1/2-inch **GOLD #2** square; press. Sew the Step 2 units to the side edges of the star block; press.

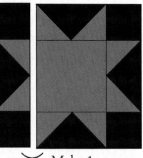

Make 1

Step 4 ✎ Aligning long edges, sew together the 2-1/2-inch wide **RED #1** strips and the 1-1/2-inch wide **BEIGE** strips; press. Crosscut the strip set into segments.

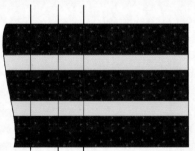

Crosscut 4, 2-1/2-inch wide segments

Step 5 ✎ Sew 2-1/2-inch **DARK BLUE** squares to both side edges of 2 of the Step 4 pieced border units; press.

Make 2

Step 6 ✎ Sew 2 of the Step 4 pieced border units to the top and bottom edges of the star block; press. Sew the Step 5 units to the side edges of the star block; press. *At this point the block should measure 12-1/2-inches square.*

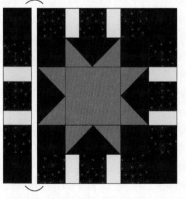

MONTH BY MONTH Block 7

MONTH *by* MONTH
BLOCK 8 - *August*

CUTTING

From DARK BROWN PRINT:
❋ Cut 1, 4-1/2-inch square

From GOLD PRINT #1:
❋ Cut 1, 2-1/2 x 42-inch strip.
  From the strip cut:
    8, 2-1/2-inch squares
    4, 1-1/2-inch squares

From MEDIUM BROWN PRINT:
❋ Cut 2, 2-1/2 x 42-inch strips.
  From the strips cut:
    12, 2-1/2-inch squares
    4, 2-1/2 x 4-1/2-inch rectangles

From GREEN PRINT #1:
❋ Cut 4, 2-1/2-inch squares

From BEIGE PRINT:
❋ Cut 1, 2-1/2 x 42-inch strip.
  From the strip cut:
    8, 2-1/2-inch squares
    4, 2-1/2 x 4-1/2-inch rectangles

PIECING

Step 1 ✒ With right sides together, position 1-1/2-inch **GOLD #1** squares on the corners of the 4-1/2-inch **DARK BROWN** square. Draw a diagonal line on the **GOLD #1** squares; stitch, trim, and press.

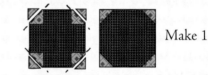

Make 1

Step 2 ✒ With right sides together, position a 2-1/2-inch **MEDIUM BROWN** square on the corner of a 2-1/2 x 4-1/2-inch **BEIGE** rectangle. Draw a diagonal line on the square; stitch, trim, and press. Repeat this process at the opposite corner of the rectangle.

Make 4

Step 3 ✒ Sew 2-1/2-inch **BEIGE** squares to both side edges of 2 of the Step 2 units. Sew 2-1/2-inch **GREEN #1** squares to both side edges of the units; press.

Make 2

Step 4 ✂ With right sides together, position a 2-1/2-inch **GOLD #1** square on the corner of a 2-1/2 x 4-1/2-inch **MEDIUM BROWN** rectangle. Draw a diagonal line on the **GOLD #1** square; stitch, trim, and press. Repeat this process at the opposite corner of the rectangle.

Make 4

Step 5 ✂ Sew 2-1/2-inch **MEDIUM BROWN** squares to both side edges of 2 of the Step 4 units. Sew 2-1/2-inch **BEIGE** squares to both side edges of the units; press.

Make 2

Step 6 ✂ Sew Step 4 units to both side edges of the Step 1 flower center. Sew Step 2 units to both side edges of this unit; press.

Make 1

Step 7 ✂ Sew together the units from Step 3, 5, and 6; press. *At this point the block should measure 12-1/2-inches square.*

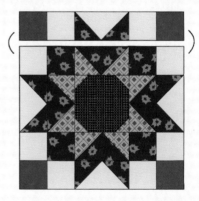

MONTH BY MONTH Block 8

MONTH *by* MONTH
BLOCK 9 - *September*

CUTTING

From RED PRINT #3:
❋ Cut 1, 4-1/2 x 8-1/2-inch rectangle
❋ Cut 2, 3-1/2 x 4-1/2-inch rectangles
❋ Cut 1, 1-1/2 x 20-inch strip.
   From the strip cut:
      2, 1-1/2 x 4-1/2-inch rectangles
      3, 1-1/2 x 2-1/2-inch rectangles

From GREEN PRINT #2:
❋ Cut 2, 4-1/2-inch squares

From DARK BROWN PRINT:
❋ Cut 1, 2 x 6-1/2-inch rectangle
❋ Cut 1, 2-1/2 x 3-1/2-inch rectangle
❋ Cut 1, 2-1/2-inch square

From GOLD PRINT #1:
❋ Cut 6, 1-1/2 x 2-1/2-inch rectangles

From GREEN PRINT #3:
❋ Cut 6, 1-1/2 x 2-1/2-inch rectangles

From BEIGE PRINT:
❋ Cut 1, 4-1/2-inch square
❋ Cut 1, 3 x 6-1/2-inch rectangle
❋ Cut 1, 2-1/2 x 8-1/2-inch rectangle

PIECING

Step 1 ✐ With right sides together, position the 4-1/2-inch **BEIGE** square on the left corner of the 4-1/2 x 8-1/2-inch **RED #3** rectangle. Draw a diagonal line on the square; stitch, trim, and press. Position a 4-1/2-inch **GREEN #2** square on the opposite corner of the rectangle. Draw a diagonal line on the square; stitch, trim, and press. Sew the 2-1/2 x 8-1/2-inch **BEIGE** rectangle to the top edge of this unit; press.

Make 1

Step 2 ✐ Sew together the 2 x 6-1/2-inch **DARK BROWN** rectangle and the 3 x 6-1/2-inch **BEIGE** rectangle; press. Position a 4-1/2-inch **GREEN #2** square on the lower edge of this unit. Draw a diagonal line on the square; stitch, trim, and press.

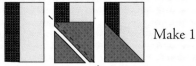

Make 1

Step 3 ✂ Sew together the units from Step 1 and Step 2; press. *At this point the unit should measure 6-1/2 x 12-1/2-inches.*

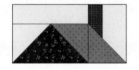

Make 1

Step 4 ✂ Sew the 1-1/2 x 2-1/2-inch **RED #3** rectangle to the top edge of the 2-1/2 x 3-1/2-inch **DARK BROWN** rectangle; press. Sew the remaining 1-1/2 x 2-1/2-inch **RED #3** rectangles to the top and bottom edges of the 2-1/2-inch **DARK BROWN** square; press.

Door   Window

Step 5 ✂ Sew the 3-1/2 x 4-1/2-inch **RED #3** rectangles to both side edges of the door unit; press. Sew the 1-1/2 x 4-1/2-inch **RED #3** rectangles to both side edges of the window unit; press. Sew these units together; press. *At this point the unit should measure 4-1/2 x 12-1/2-inches.*

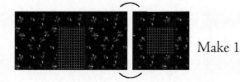

Make 1

Step 6 ✂ Sew together the 1-1/2 x 2-1/2-inch **GOLD #1** and **GREEN #3** rectangles; press.

Make 1

Step 7 ✂ Sew together the units from Step 3, Step 5, and Step 6; press. *At this point the block should measure 12-1/2-inches square.*

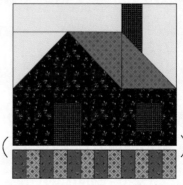

MONTH BY MONTH Block 9

41

MONTH *by* MONTH
BLOCK 10 - *October*

CUTTING

From ORANGE #1, #2, and #3 PRINTS:
※ Cut 1, 5-1/2 x 6-1/2-inch rectangle from each fabric

From GREEN PRINT #2:
※ Cut 1, 2-7/8 x 42-inch strip.
From the strip cut:
1, 2-7/8-inch square
1, 2-1/2 x 6-1/2-inch rectangle
1, 2-1/2 x 4-1/2-inch rectangle
1, 2-1/2-inch square
1, 1 x 4-inch strip

From GREEN PRINT #1:
※ Cut 3, 1-1/2-inch squares

From BEIGE PRINT:
※ Cut 1, 2-7/8 x 18-inch strip.
From the strip cut:
1, 2-7/8-inch square
1, 2-5/8-inch square
4, 2-1/2-inch squares
※ Cut 1, 1-1/2 x 42-inch strip.
From the strip cut:
1, 1-1/2 x 6-1/2-inch rectangle
2, 1-1/2 x 4-1/2-inch rectangles
2, 1-1/2 x 2-1/2-inch rectangles
12, 1-1/2-inch squares

PIECING

Step 1 ✍ With right sides together, position 1-1/2-inch **BEIGE** squares on the 4 corners of the 5-1/2 x 6-1/2-inch **ORANGE #1** rectangle. Draw a diagonal line on the squares; stitch, trim, and press. Repeat this process using the 5-1/2 x 6-1/2-inch **ORANGE #2** and #3 rectangles.

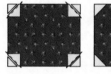

Make 1 pumpkin square from **ORANGE #1, #2,** and **#3**

Step 2 ✍ With right sides together, position a 1-1/2-inch **GREEN #1** square on the corner of a 1-1/2 x 4-1/2-inch **BEIGE** rectangle. Draw a diagonal line on the square; stitch, trim, and press. Repeat this process using the 1-1/2 x 6-1/2-inch **BEIGE** rectangle.

Make 2

Make 1

Step 3 ✏ Sew a 1-1/2 x 2-1/2-inch **BEIGE** rectangle to the right edge of one of the 1-1/2 x 4-1/2-inch stem units; press. Sew this unit to the top edge of the **ORANGE #1** pumpkin.

Make 1

Step 4 ✏ Sew together the remaining 1-1/2 x 4-1/2-inch stem unit, the 1-1/2 x 6-1/2-inch stem unit, and a 1-1/2 x 2-1/2-inch **BEIGE** rectangle; press. Sew the **ORANGE #2** and **ORANGE #3** pumpkins together; press. Sew the stem unit to the top edge of the pumpkin unit; press. *At this point the unit should measure 6-1/2 x 12-1/2-inches.*

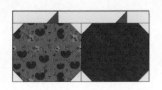

Step 5 ✏ With right sides together, layer the 2-7/8-inch **GREEN #2** and **BEIGE** squares. Cut the layered square in half diagonally. Stitch 1/4-inch from the diagonal edge of each pair of triangles; press. Sew the triangle-pieced squares together; press. Sew the 2-1/2-inch **GREEN #2** square to the right edge of the unit; press.

Make 2, 2-1/2-inch   Make 1
triangle-pieced squares

Step 6 ✏ With right sides together, position 2-1/2-inch **BEIGE** squares on the corners of the 2-1/2 x 6-1/2-inch **GREEN #2** rectangle. Draw a diagonal line on the squares; stitch, trim, and press.

Make 1

(continued on the next page)

Step 7 ✎ With right sides together, position a 2-1/2-inch **BEIGE** square on the corner of the 2-1/2 x 4-1/2-inch **GREEN #2** rectangle. Draw a diagonal line on the square; stitch, trim, and press. Position the remaining 2-1/2-inch **BEIGE** square on the opposite corner of the rectangle. Draw a diagonal line on the square; stitch, trim, and press.

Make 1

Step 8 ✎ Cut the 2-5/8-inch **BEIGE** square in half diagonally. Center a **BEIGE** triangle on the 1 x 4-inch **GREEN #2** strip. Stitch a 1/4-inch seam, and press the seam allowance toward the **GREEN** strip. Repeat on the other side of the **GREEN** strip; press. The stem will extend beyond the triangles. Trim the ends of the stem so that the unit measures 2-1/2-inches square. Sew the stem unit to the Step 7 unit; press.

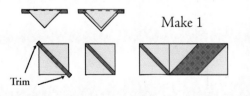

Make 1

Trim

Step 9 ✎ Sew together the units from Steps 5, 6, and 8; press. Sew the leaf unit to the left edge of the **ORANGE #1** pumpkin; press. *At this point the unit should measure 6-1/2 x 12-1/2-inches.*

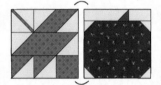

Step 10 ✎ Sew together the units from Step 4 and Step 9; press. *At this point the block should measure 12-1/2-inches square.*

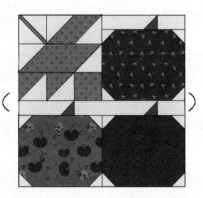

MONTH BY MONTH Block 10

CUTTING

From MEDIUM BROWN PRINT:

❋ Cut 1, 2-7/8 x 42-strip.
  From the strip cut:
    10, 2-7/8-inch squares

From GREEN PRINT #1:

❋ Cut 1, 2-1/2 x 20-inch strip.
  From the strip cut:
    4, 2-1/2 x 4-1/2-inch rectangles

From LIGHT GOLD PRINT:

❋ Cut 1, 2-1/2 x 22-inch strip.
  From the strip cut:
    8, 2-1/2-inch squares

From BEIGE PRINT:

❋ Cut 1, 2-7/8 x 42-inch strip.
  From the strip cut:
    10, 2-7/8-inch squares

PIECING

Step 1 ✎ With right sides together, layer the 2-7/8-inch **MEDIUM BROWN** and **BEIGE** squares together in pairs. Cut the layered squares in half diagonally to make 20 sets of layered triangles. Stitch 1/4-inch from the diagonal edge of each pair of triangles; press.

 Make 20, 2-1/2-inch triangle-pieced squares

Step 2 ✎ Sew 4 triangle-pieced squares together for each sawtooth border; press.

Make 4

Step 3 ✎ Sew 2-1/2-inch **LIGHT GOLD** squares to both side edges of 2 of the Step 2 units; press. *At this point each unit should measure 2-1/2 x 12-1/2-inches.*

 Make 2

Step 4 ✒ To make the pinwheel, sew the remaining triangle-pieced squares together in pairs; press. Sew the pairs together; press. *At this point the pinwheel should measure 4-1/2-inches square.*

) Make 1

Step 5 ✒ Sew 2-1/2 x 4-1/2-inch **GREEN #1** rectangles to the top and bottom edges of the Step 4 pinwheel; press. Sew 2-1/2-inch **LIGHT GOLD** squares to both side edges of the remaining **GREEN #1** rectangles; press. Sew the strips to the side edges of the pinwheel; press. Sew the remaining sawtooth borders to the side edge of the unit; press. *At this point the unit should measure 8-1/2 x 12-1/2-inches.*

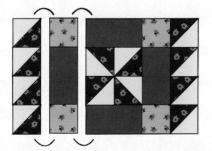

Step 6 ✒ Sew the Step 3 units to the top and bottom edges of the Step 5 unit; press. *At this point the block should measure 12-1/2-inches square.*

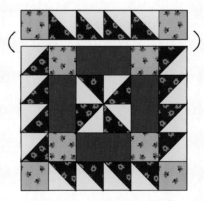

MONTH BY MONTH Block 11

MONTH *by* MONTH
BLOCK 12 - *December*

CUTTING

From GREEN PRINT #2:
✵ Cut 1, 4-1/2 x 42-inch strip.
   From the strip cut:
      1, 4-1/2 x 8-1/2-inch rectangle
      1, 4-1/2 x 12-1/2-inch rectangle
      1, 2-1/2 x 12-1/2-inch rectangle

From RED PRINT #3:
✵ Cut 1, 2-1/2 x 8-1/2-inch rectangle

From BEIGE PRINT:
✵ Cut 1, 4-1/2 x 42-inch strip.
   From the strip cut:
      2, 4-1/2 x 6-1/2-inch rectangles
      2, 4-1/2-inch squares
      2, 2-1/2-inch squares
      2, 2-1/2 x 4-1/2-inch rectangles

PIECING

Step 1 ✍ With right sides together, position a 4-1/2 x 6-1/2-inch **BEIGE** rectangle on the left edge of the 4-1/2 x 8-1/2-inch **GREEN #2** rectangle. Draw a diagonal line on the **BEIGE** rectangle; stitch, trim, and press. Repeat this process on the opposite corner of the **GREEN #2** rectangle. *At this point the unit should measure 4-1/2 x 12-1/2-inches.*

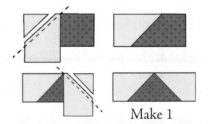

Make 1

Step 2 ✍ With right sides together, position 4-1/2-inch **BEIGE** squares on the corners of the 4-1/2 x 12-1/2-inch **GREEN #2** rectangle. Draw a diagonal line on the squares; stitch, trim, and press. *At this point the unit should measure 4-1/2 x 12-1/2-inches.*

Make 1

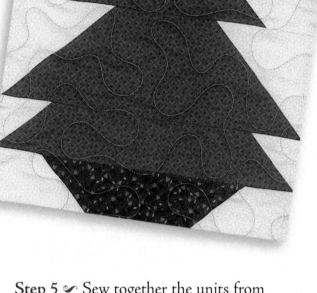

Step 3 ✒ With right sides together, position 2-1/2-inch **BEIGE** squares on the corners of the 2-1/2 x 12-1/2-inch **GREEN #2** rectangle. Draw a diagonal line on the squares; stitch, trim, and press. *At this point the unit should measure 2-1/2 x 12-1/2-inches.*

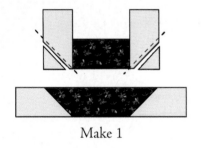

Make 1

Step 4 ✒ With right sides together, position 2-1/2 x 4-1/2-inch **BEIGE** rectangles on the corners of the 2-1/2 x 8-1/2-inch **RED #3** rectangle. Draw a diagonal line on the **BEIGE** rectangles; stitch, trim, and press. *At this point the unit should measure 2-1/2 x 12-1/2-inches.*

Make 1

Step 5 ✒ Sew together the units from Steps 1 through 4. Press the seam allowances toward the tree base. *At this point the block should measure 12-1/2-inches square.*

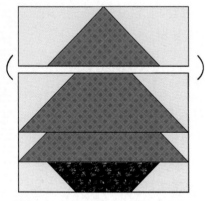

Month by Month Block 12

49

FINISHING THE QUILT

QUILT CENTER

CUTTING

From the 18 ASSORTED PRINTS:

❋ Cut a total of 48, 2-1/2 x 17-inch block border strips. It is a good idea to cut extra block border strips so you can move them around to get just the coloration you are looking for.

QUILT CENTER ASSEMBLY

Step 1 ❧ Referring to the quilt diagram for block placement, lay out the 12 blocks. Lay the **ASSORTED PRINT** block border strips around each block.

Step 2 ❧ Working with 1 block at a time, sew the top border strip to the block. Press the seam allowances toward the border strip. Trim the strip even with the block. Sew the border strip to the left edge of the block; press and trim. Sew the bottom border strip to the block; press and trim. Sew the border strip to the right edge of the block; press and trim. *At this point the block should measure 16-1/2-inches square.*

Step 3 ❧ Repeat Step 2 to add the block borders to each of the blocks.

Step 4 ❧ Referring to the quilt diagram for block placement, sew the blocks together in 4 rows with 3 blocks each. Press the seam allowances in alternating directions by rows so the seams will fit together snugly with less bulk.

Step 5 ❧ Pin the rows together at the block intersections and sew together. Press the seam allowances in one direction.

BORDERS

NOTE: *The yardage given allows for the border strips to be cut on the crosswise grain. Diagonally piece the strips as needed, referring to **Binding Basics** instructions on page 253. Read through **Border** instructions on page 250, for general instructions on adding borders.*

CUTTING

From GOLD PRINT #3:
❈ Cut 6, 1-1/2 x 42-inch inner border strips

From GREEN/RUST FLORAL:
❈ Cut 7, 6-1/2 x 42-inch outer border strips

ATTACHING THE BORDERS

Step 1 ❧ Attach the 1-1/2-inch wide **GOLD PRINT #3** inner border strips.

Step 2 ❧ Attach the 6-1/2-inch wide **GREEN/RUST FLORAL** outer border strips.

PUTTING IT ALL TOGETHER

❈ Cut the 4-2/3 yard length of backing fabric in half crosswise to make 2, 2-1/3 yard lengths. Refer to **Quilting the Project** on page 252 for complete instructions.

BINDING

From GREEN PRINT #2:
❈ Cut 8, 2-3/4 x 42-inch strips

Sew the binding to the quilt using a 3/8-inch seam allowance. This measurement will produce a 1/2-inch wide finished binding. Refer to **Binding** and **Diagonal Piecing** on page 253 for complete instructions.

THIMBLEBERRIES®
VILLAGE™

Celebrating the warmth and charm of small town America, this quilt will walk with you down memory lane.

THIMBLEBERRIES® VILLAGE is my second 12-block quilt series. This finished quilt allows the quilter and all who see it to imagine the village of their dreams. Is it a small town in the heartland? Is it a New England town square? For some, it might evoke memories of a summer spent in a small, lakeside town. Of course, the beauty of this quilt is what it means to you! Included in THIMBLEBERRIES® VILLAGE are blocks for Main Street Manor, Summer Cottage, Lakeside and Log Cabin Lane. Several of these blocks— especially Blossom Time, Log Cabin Lane and Starlight—are wonderful blocks all by themselves, perfect for table runners, pillows or wall hangings. The collage of blocks in THIMBLEBERRIES® VILLAGE are non-linear and of different sizes. The result is to suggest a village feeling. These blocks work wonderfully as individual projects or collectively as a large quilt, perfect for the bedroom.

Enjoy your own THIMBLEBERRIES® VILLAGE.

THIMBLEBERRIES®
VILLAGE

✂

80 x 102 inches

Fabrics & Supplies

3-1/2 yards
BEIGE PRINT
for all 12 blocks, inner border

5/8 yard
GOLD PRINT
for blocks 1, 5, 10, 12

5/8 yard
MEDIUM BLUE PRINT
for blocks 1, 6, 9

1/2 yard
DARK GOLD PRINT
for blocks 2, 6, 8

1/3 yard
GOLD STAR PRINT
for blocks 2, 9

1/2 yard
GOLD/BLACK PLAID
for blocks 2, 7, 12

1/2 yard
RED DIAGONAL PRINT
for blocks 3, 6, 7, 12

1/4 yard
DARK GREEN PRINT
for blocks 3, 6

2-1/4 yards
GREEN FLORAL
for blocks 3, 9, 10, outer border

1/8 yard
GREEN PLAID
for block 3

8" x 20" piece
CHESTNUT PRINT
for block 5

5/8 yard
GREEN TREE PRINT
for blocks 4, 6, 12

5/8 yard **BROWN
DIAGONAL PRINT**
for blocks 5, 6, 7, 9, 10, 12

1/3 yard
CHESTNUT FLORAL
for blocks 4, 6, 9, 12

3/8 yard
GREEN/ROSE FLORAL
for blocks 6, 7, 8, 10

5/8 yard
BLUE FLORAL
for blocks 5, 6, 10, 11

1-1/4 yards **RED PRINT**
for blocks 6, 7, 9, 11,
first middle border

6" x 42" piece
DARK RUST PRINT
for block 5

1/3 yard
RED FLORAL
for blocks 6, 8, 10

1/3 yard
BROWN PRINT
for blocks 6, 7

5/8 yard
BLACK PRINT
for block 8, second middle border

1/2 yard
DARK BLUE PRINT
for blocks 6, 11

6" x 12" piece
PURPLE PRINT
for block 10

6" x 42" piece
LIGHT GOLD PRINT
for block 7

7/8 yard
**BROWN DIAGONAL
PRINT**
for binding

1/4 yard
**GREEN DIAGONAL
PRINT** for block 8

7 yards backing fabric
quilt batting,
at least 84 x 106-inches

Before beginning this project, read through **Getting Started** on page 244.

*This fabric key should be used as a helpful guideline in selecting fabric for your quilt project.
We cannot guarantee that a specific fabric will be available at your favorite quilt store,
but suitable substitutions can be found.*

THIMBLEBERRIES® VILLAGE
BLOCK I - *Sunshine*

CUTTING

From GOLD PRINT:
❈ Cut 1, 4-1/2 x 20-inch strip.
 From the strip cut:
  1, 4-1/2-inch square
  2, 2-7/8-inch squares
❈ Cut 3, 2-1/2 x 20-inch strips.
 From the strips cut:
  4, 2-1/2 x 4-1/2-inch rectangles
  16, 2-1/2-inch squares

From BEIGE PRINT:
❈ Cut 3, 2-1/2 x 42-inch strips.
 From the strips cut:
  3, 2-1/2 x 16-inch strips
  8, 2-1/2 x 4-1/2-inch rectangles
  8, 2-1/2-inch squares
❈ Cut 2, 2-7/8-inch squares

From MEDIUM BLUE PRINT:
❈ Cut 3, 2-1/2 x 16-inch strips

PIECING

Step 1 ✌ Position a 2-1/2-inch **GOLD** square on the corner of a 2-1/2 x 4-1/2-inch **BEIGE** rectangle. Draw a diagonal line on the square and stitch on the line. Trim the seam allowance to 1/4-inch; press. Repeat this process at the opposite corner of the rectangle. Sew the units together in pairs; press. *At this point each unit should measure 4-1/2-inches square.*

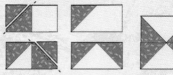

Make 8   Make 4

Step 2 ✌ Position a 2-1/2-inch **BEIGE** square on the left corner of a 2-1/2 x 4-1/2-inch **GOLD** rectangle. Draw a diagonal line on the square and stitch, trim, press.

 Make 2

Step 3 ✌ Position a 2-1/2-inch **BEIGE** square on the right corner of a 2-1/2 x 4-1/2-inch **GOLD** rectangle. Draw a diagonal line on the square and stitch, trim, press.

 Make 2

Step 4 ✍ With right sides together, layer the 2-7/8-inch **GOLD** and **BEIGE** squares in pairs. Press together but do not sew. Cut the layered squares in half diagonally to make 4 sets of layered triangles. Stitch 1/4-inch from the diagonal edge of each pair of triangles; press. *At this point each triangle-pieced square should measure 2-1/2-inches square.*

Make 4, 2-1/2-inch triangle-pieced squares

Step 5 ✍ Sew a 2-1/2-inch **BEIGE** square to each triangle-pieced square, referring to the diagrams for placement. Sew the Step 2 and 3 units to the bottom edges of the units; press. *At this point each unit should measure 4-1/2-inches square.*

Make 2   Make 2

(continued on the next page)

Step 6 ✑ Sew the Step 5 units to 2 of the Step 1 units; press. Sew the remaining Step 1 units to the side edges of the 4-1/2-inch **GOLD** square; press. Sew the rows together; press. *At this point the block should measure 12-1/2-inches square.*

Make 1

Step 7 ✑ Aligning long edges, sew 2-1/2 x 16-inch **MEDIUM BLUE** strips to the top and bottom edges of a 2-1/2 x 16-inch **BEIGE** strip; press. Cut the strip set into segments.

Crosscut 6, 2-1/2-inch wide segments

Step 8 ✑ Aligning long edges, sew 2-1/2 x 16-inch **BEIGE** strips to the top and bottom edges of a 2-1/2 x 16-inch **MEDIUM BLUE** strip; press. Cut the strip set into segments.

Crosscut 6, 2-1/2-inch wide segments

Step 9 ✑ Sew the Step 7 and Step 8 segments together as diagramed; press. *At this point the checkerboard unit should measure 6-1/2 x 12-1/2-inches.*

Make 2

Step 10 ✑ Sew the Step 9 units to both side edges of the Step 6 block; press. *At this point the block should measure 12-1/2 x 24-1/2-inches.*

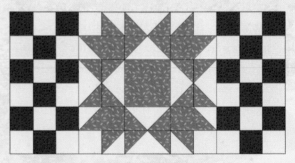

THIMBLEBERRIES VILLAGE Block 1

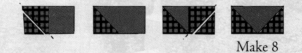

THIMBLEBERRIES® VILLAGE
BLOCK TWO - *Starlight*

CUTTING

From DARK GOLD PRINT:
❋ Cut 2, 2-1/2 x 42-inch strips.
   From the strips cut:
      16, 2-1/2-inch squares
      8, 2-1/2 x 4-1/2-inch rectangles
❋ Cut 2, 4-1/2-inch squares

From GOLD STAR PRINT:
❋ Cut 1, 4-1/2 x 20-inch strip.
   From the strip cut:
      1, 4-1/2-inch square
      4, 2-1/2 x 4-1/2-inch rectangles
❋ Cut 1, 2-1/2 x 20-inch strip.
   From the strip cut:
      8, 2-1/2-inch squares

From GOLD/BLACK PLAID:
❋ Cut 2, 2-1/2 x 42-inch strips.
   From the strips cut:
      24, 2-1/2-inch squares

From BEIGE PRINT:
❋ Cut 3, 4-1/2 x 42-inch strips.
   From the strips cut:
      12, 4-1/2-inch squares
      12, 2-1/2 x 4-1/2-inch rectangles

PIECING

Step 1 ❧ Position a 2-1/2-inch **DARK GOLD** square on the corner of a 2-1/2 x 4-1/2-inch **BEIGE** rectangle. Draw a diagonal line on the square, stitch, trim, and press. Repeat this process at the opposite corner of the rectangle.

Make 8

Step 2 ❧ Position a 2-1/2-inch **GOLD/BLACK PLAID** square on the corner of a 2-1/2 x 4-1/2-inch **DARK GOLD** rectangle. Draw a diagonal line on the square; stitch, trim, and press. Repeat this process at the opposite corner of the rectangle.

Make 8

Step 3 ❧ Sew the Step 1 and Step 2 units together in pairs; press. *At this point each unit should measure 4-1/2-inches square.*

Make 8

(continued on the next page)

Step 4 ✔ Sew Step 3 units to the top and bottom edges of the 4-1/2-inch **DARK GOLD** squares; press. Sew 4-1/2-inch **BEIGE** squares to the remaining Step 3 units; press. Sew the units together to make 2 stars; press. *At this point each star should measure 12-1/2-inches square.*

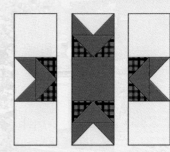

Make 2   Make 2   Make 2

Step 5 ✔ Position a 2 1/2-inch **GOLD STAR PRINT** square on the corner of a 2-1/2 x 4-1/2-inch **BEIGE** rectangle. Draw a diagonal line on the square; stitch, trim, and press. Repeat this process at the opposite corner of the rectangle.

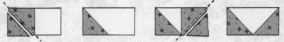

Make 4

Step 6 ✔ Position a 2-1/2-inch **GOLD/BLACK PLAID** square on the corner of a 2-1/2 x 4-1/2-inch **GOLD STAR PRINT** rectangle. Draw a diagonal line on the square; stitch, trim, and press. Repeat this process at the opposite corner of the rectangle.

Make 4

Step 7 ✔ Sew the Step 5 and Step 6 units together in pairs; press. *At this point each unit should measure 4-1/2-inches square.*

Make 4

Step 8 ❧ Sew Step 7 units to the top and bottom edges of the 4-1/2-inch **GOLD STAR PRINT** square; press. Sew 4-1/2-inch **BEIGE** squares to the remaining Step 7 units; press. Sew the units together to make 1 star; press. *At this point the star should measure 12-1/2-inches square.*

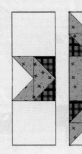 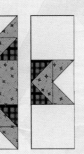

Make 1   Make 1   Make 1

Step 9 ❧ Sew a Step 4 star to both side edges of the Step 8 star; press. *At this point the block should measure 12-1/2 x 36-1/2-inches.*

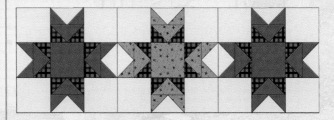

THIMBLEBERRIES VILLAGE Block 2

THIMBLEBERRIES® VILLAGE
BLOCK 3- *Apple Orchard*

CUTTING

From RED DIAGONAL PRINT:
❋ Cut 1, 4-1/2 x 42-inch strip.
  From the strip cut:
    3, 4-1/2-inch squares
    4, 2-1/2-inch squares

From BEIGE PRINT:
❋ Cut 2, 2-1/2 x 42-inch strips.
  From the strips cut:
    3, 2-1/2 x 6-1/2-inch rectangles
    13, 2-1/2-inch squares
    12, 1-1/2-inch squares
❋ Cut 1, 2-7/8 x 42-inch strip.
  From the strip cut:
    7, 2-7/8-inch squares
    4, 2-5/8-inch squares

From DARK GREEN PRINT:
❋ Cut 1, 2-7/8 x 10-inch strip.
  From the strip cut:
    3, 2-7/8-inch squares

From GREEN FLORAL:
❋ Cut 1, 2-1/2 x 42-inch strip.
  From the strip cut:
    3, 2-1/2 x 6-1/2-inch rectangles
    3, 2-1/2 x 4-1/2-inch rectangles
❋ Cut 1, 2-7/8 x 42-inch strip.
  From the strip cut:
    3, 2-7/8-inch squares
    3, 2-1/2-inch squares
    3, 1 x 4-inch strips

From GREEN PLAID:
❋ Cut 1, 2-7/8 x 42-inch strip.
  From the strip cut:
    1, 2-7/8-inch square
    1, 2-1/2-inch square
    1, 2-1/2 x 6-1/2-inch rectangle
    1, 2-1/2 x 4-1/2-inch rectangle
    1, 1 x 4-inch strip

PIECING

Step 1 ✿ Position 1-1/2-inch **BEIGE** squares on the corners of the 4-1/2-inch **RED DIAGONAL PRINT** squares. Draw a diagonal line on the **BEIGE** squares, and stitch on the lines. Trim the seam allowance to 1/4-inch; press.

 Make 3

Step 2 ✿ With right sides together, layer 3, 2-7/8-inch **BEIGE** and **DARK GREEN** squares together in pairs. Cut the layered squares in half diagonally to make 6 sets of layered triangles. Press together, but do not sew. Stitch 1/4-inch from the diagonal edge of each pair of triangles; press. Sew the triangle-pieced squares together in pairs; press.

Make 6, 2-1/2-inch triangle-pieced squares

 Make 2  Make 1

Step 3 ✿ Sew the Step 2 units to each of the Step 1 units; press. Sew 2-1/2 x 6-1/2-inch **BEIGE** rectangles to the units; press. *At this point each block should measure 6-1/2-inches square.*

Make 2   Make 1

(continued on the next page)

65

Step 4 ✂ Sew 2-1/2-inch **BEIGE** squares to both side edges of 2 of the 2-1/2-inch **RED DIAGONAL PRINT** squares; press. Sew the remaining 2-1/2-inch **RED DIAGONAL PRINT** squares to both side edges of a 2-1/2-inch **BEIGE** square; press. Sew the units together; press. *At this point the block should measure 6-1/2-inches square.*

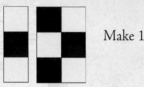

Make 1

Step 5 ✂ Position a 2-1/2-inch **BEIGE** square on the right corner of a 2-1/2 x 6-1/2-inch **GREEN FLORAL** rectangle. Draw a diagonal line on the square; stitch, trim, and press.

Make 3

Step 6 ✂ Position a 2-1/2-inch **BEIGE** square on the right corner of a 2-1/2 x 4-1/2-inch **GREEN FLORAL** rectangle. Draw a diagonal line on the square, stitch, trim, and press.

Make 3

Step 7 ✂ With right sides together, layer 3, 2-7/8-inch **BEIGE** and **GREEN FLORAL** squares together in pairs. Press together, but do not sew. Cut the layered squares in half diagonally to make 6 sets of layered triangles. Stitch 1/4-inch from the diagonal edge of each pair of triangles; press. Sew the triangle-pieced squares together in pairs; press. Sew a 2-1/2-inch **GREEN FLORAL** square to the right edge of each of the units; press.

Make 6, 2-1/2-inch triangle-pieced squares

Make 3

Step 8 ✂ Cut the 2-5/8-inch **BEIGE** square in half diagonally. Center a **BEIGE** triangle on the 1 x 4-inch **GREEN FLORAL** strip; stitch. Center another **BEIGE** triangle on the **GREEN FLORAL** strip; stitch and press. The stem will extend beyond the triangles. Trim the ends of the stem so that the unit measures 2-1/2-inches square. Sew the stem unit to the Step 6 unit; press.

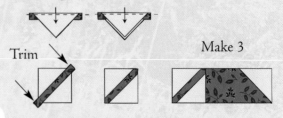

Trim

Make 3

Step 9 ✒ Sew together the Step 5, Step 7, and Step 8 units; press. *At this point each block should measure 6-1/2-inches square.*

Make 3

Step 10 ✒ Repeat Steps 5 through 9 using the **GREEN PLAID** pieces and the remaining **BEIGE** pieces to make one leaf block. *At this point the block should measure 6-1/2-inches square.*

Make 1

Step 11 ✒ Sew the Step 3, Step 4, Step 9, and Step 10 units together in horizontal rows; press. Sew the rows together; press. *At this point the block should measure 12-1/2 x 24-1/2-inches.*

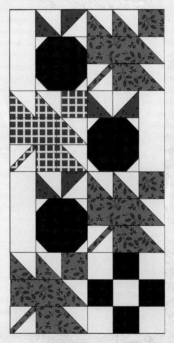

THIMBLEBERRIES VILLAGE Block 3

67

THIMBLEBERRIES® VILLAGE
BLOCK 4 - *White Pine*

CUTTING

From GREEN TREE PRINT:

❄ Cut 1, 4-1/2 x 42-inch strip.
  From the strip cut:
    2, 4-1/2 x 12-1/2-inch rectangles
    2, 4-1/2-inch squares

❄ Cut 2, 2-1/2 x 42-inch strips.
  From the strips cut:
    3, 2-1/2 x 8-1/2-inch rectangles
    2, 2-1/2 x 12-1/2-inch rectangles

From BEIGE PRINT:

❄ Cut 1, 4-1/2 x 42-inch strip.
  From the strip cut:
    2, 4-1/2 x 6-1/2-inch rectangles
    4, 4-1/2-inch squares
    4, 2-1/2-inch squares

❄ Cut 1, 2-1/2 x 42-inch strip.
  From the strip cut:
    8, 2-1/2 x 4-1/2-inch rectangles

From CHESTNUT FLORAL:

❄ Cut 1, 2-1/2 x 4-1/2-inch rectangle

PIECING

Step 1 ↝ Position a 4-1/2-inch **GREEN TREE PRINT** square on the right corner of a 4-1/2 x 6-1/2-inch **BEIGE** rectangle. Draw a diagonal line on the square; stitch, trim, and press.

 Make 1

Step 2 ↝ Position a 4-1/2-inch **GREEN TREE PRINT** square on the left corner of a 4-1/2 x 6-1/2-inch **BEIGE** rectangle. Draw a diagonal line on the square; stitch, trim, and press.

 Make 1

Step 3 ↝ Sew the Step 1 and Step 2 units together; press. *At this point the unit should measure 4-1/2 x 12-1/2-inches.*

 Make 1

Step 4 ↝ Position 4-1/2-inch **BEIGE** squares on the corners of the 4-1/2 x 12-1/2-inch **GREEN TREE PRINT** rectangles. Draw a diagonal line on the squares; stitch, trim, and press. *At this point each unit should measure 4-1/2 x 12-1/2-inches.*

 Make 2

Step 5 ✐ Position 2-1/2-inch **BEIGE** squares on the corners of the 2-1/2 x 12-1/2-inch **GREEN TREE PRINT** rectangles. Draw a diagonal line on the squares; stitch, trim, and press. *At this point each unit should measure 2-1/2 x 12-1/2-inches.*

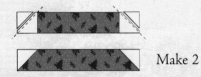

Make 2

Step 6 ✐ Position 2-1/2 x 4-1/2-inch **BEIGE** rectangles on the corners of the 2-1/2 x 8-1/2-inch **GREEN TREE PRINT** rectangles. Draw a diagonal line on the **BEIGE** rectangles; stitch, trim, and press. *At this point each unit should measure 2-1/2 x 12-1/2-inches.*

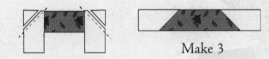

Make 3

Step 7 ✐ Sew 2-1/2 x 4-1/2-inch **BEIGE** rectangles to both side edges of the 2-1/2 x 4-1/2-inch **CHESTNUT FLORAL** rectangle; press. *At this point the unit should measure 2-1/2 x 12-1/2-inches.*

Make 1

Step 8 ✐ Sew the units from Step 3 through Step 7 together; press. *At this point the block should measure 12-1/2 x 24-1/2-inches.*

THIMBLEBERRIES VILLAGE Block 4

Thimbleberries® Village
Block 5 - *Main Street Manor*

Cutting

From BLUE FLORAL:
❄ Cut 1, 6-1/2 x 42-inch strip.
   From the strip cut:
      2, 6-1/2-inch squares
      1, 4-1/2 x 20-1/2-inch rectangle
      2, 2-1/2 x 4-1/2-inch rectangles
❄ Cut 1, 2-1/2 x 42-inch strip.
   From the strip cut:
      2, 2-1/2 x 14-1/2-inch rectangles
      2, 2-1/2 x 4-1/2-inch rectangles

From GOLD PRINT:
❄ Cut 1, 4-1/2 x 42-inch strip.
   From the strip cut:
      2, 4-1/2 x 6-1/2-inch rectangles
      2, 4-1/2-inch squares
      1, 2-1/2 x 4-1/2-inch rectangle

From DARK RUST PRINT:
❄ Cut 1, 4-1/2 x 42-inch strip.
   From the strip cut:
      1, 4-1/2-inch square
      2, 2-1/2 x 14-1/2-inch rectangles

From BEIGE PRINT:
❄ Cut 1, 6-1/2 x 20-inch strip.
   From the strip cut:
      1, 6-1/2 x 10-1/2-inch rectangle
      1, 6-1/2-inch square
❄ Cut 1, 4-1/2 x 20-inch strip.
   From the strip cut:
      1, 4-1/2-inch square
      1, 4-1/2 x 6-1/2-inch rectangle

From CHESTNUT PRINT:
❄ Cut 1, 6-1/2 x 14-1/2-inch rectangle

From BROWN DIAGONAL PRINT:
❄ Cut 1, 4-1/2 x 20-inch strip.
   From the strip cut:
      2, 4-1/2-inch squares
      1, 4-1/2 x 8-1/2-inch rectangle

PIECING

Step 1 ✒ Sew 2-1/2 x 4-1/2-inch **BLUE FLORAL** rectangles to the top and bottom edges of the 4-1/2 x 6-1/2-inch **GOLD** rectangles. Sew 4-1/2-inch **GOLD** squares to the top edge of the units; press. *At this point each unit should measure 4-1/2 x 14-1/2-inches.*

Make 2

Step 2 ✒ Sew a 2-1/2 x 14-1/2-inch **BLUE FLORAL** rectangle to the left edge of one of the Step 1 units, and sew a 2-1/2 x 14-1/2-inch **BLUE FLORAL** rectangle to the right edge of the other Step 1 unit; press. *At this point each window unit should measure 6-1/2 x 14-1/2-inches.*

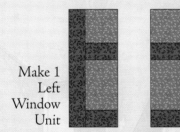

Make 1
Left
Window
Unit

Make 1
Right
Window
Unit

Step 3 ✒ Sew the 2-1/2 x 4-1/2-inch **GOLD** rectangle to the top edge of the 4-1/2 x 8-1/2-inch **BROWN DIAGONAL PRINT** rectangle. Sew the 4-1/2-inch **DARK RUST** square to the top edge of the unit; press.

Make 1

Step 4 ✒ Sew 2-1/2 x 14-1/2-inch **DARK RUST** rectangles to the side edges of the Step 3 unit; press. *At this point the unit should measure 8-1/2 x 14-1/2-inches.*

Make 1

Step 5 ✒ Position a 6-1/2-inch **BLUE FLORAL** square on the corner of the 6-1/2 x 10-1/2-inch **BEIGE** rectangle. Draw a diagonal line on the square; stitch, trim, and press.

Make 1

Step 6 ✒ Position a 6-1/2-inch **BLUE FLORAL** square on the left corner of the 6-1/2 x 14-1/2-inch **CHESTNUT** rectangle. Draw a diagonal line on the square; stitch, trim, and press. Repeat at the opposite corner of the **CHESTNUT**

71

(continued on the next page)

rectangle using a 6-1/2-inch **BEIGE** square. *At this point the unit should measure 6-1/2 x 14-1/2-inches.*

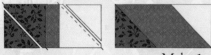

Make 1

Step 7 ❧ Sew a 4-1/2-inch **BROWN DIAGONAL PRINT** square to the top edge of the 4-1/2 x 20-1/2-inch **BLUE FLORAL** rectangle as shown in Step 9; press.

Step 8 ❧ Sew the 4-1/2-inch **BEIGE** square to the left edge of a 4-1/2-inch **BROWN DIAGONAL PRINT** square. Sew the 4-1/2 x 6-1/2-inch **BEIGE** rectangle to the opposite edge of the **BROWN DIAGONAL PRINT** square; press. Sew this unit to the top edge of the Step 6 unit; press. *At this point the roof unit should measure 10-1/2 x 14-1/2-inches.*

Make 1

Make 1

Step 9 ❧ Referring to the assembly diagram, sew the units together in sections; press. Sew the sections together; press. *At this point the block should measure 24-1/2-inches square.*

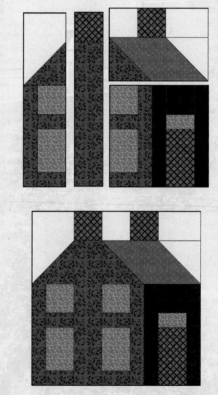

THIMBLEBERRIES VILLAGE Block 5

CUTTING

From BEIGE PRINT:

❋ Cut 3, 2-1/2 x 42-inch strips.
  From the strips cut:
    40, 2-1/2-inch squares

From each MEDIUM BLUE, RED DIAGONAL PRINT, CHESTNUT FLORAL, and GREEN/ROSE FLORAL:

❋ Cut 1, 1-1/2 x 42-inch strip
❋ Cut 1, 2-1/2 x 42-inch strip.
  From the strip cut:
    5, 2-1/2 x 4-1/2-inch rectangles
      for flying geese

From each DARK GREEN PRINT, GREEN TREE PRINT, BLUE FLORAL, BROWN DIAGONAL PRINT, RED PRINT, RED FLORAL, BROWN PRINT, and DARK BLUE PRINT:

❋ Cut 1, 1-1/2 x 42-inch strip

From DARK GOLD PRINT:

❋ Cut 2, 4-1/2-inch squares
❋ Cut 3, 2-1/2 -inch squares

PIECING

Step 1 ❧ To make the flying geese units, position a 2-1/2-inch **BEIGE** square on the corner of a 2-1/2 x 4-1/2-inch **DARK PRINT** rectangle. Draw a diagonal line on the square; stitch, trim, and press. Repeat this process at the opposite corner of the rectangle.

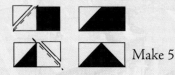 Make 5

Step 2 ❧ To make the remaining flying geese units, repeat Step 1, combining the remaining 2-1/2-inch **BEIGE** squares with the remaining 2-1/2 x 4-1/2-inch **DARK PRINT** rectangles. *At this point each flying geese unit should measure 2-1/2 x 4-1/2-inches.*

Step 3 ❧ Sew together 4 flying geese units, one of each color; press. *At this point each flying geese strip should measure 4-1/2 x 8-1/2-inches.*

 Make 5

(continued on the next page)

73

Step 4 ✎ Referring to the block diagram, sew together 3 of the Step 3 flying geese strips, and the 4-1/2-inch **DARK GOLD** squares; press. Set the remaining flying geese strips aside.

NOTE: *For a scrappy look, position the Log Cabin strips in a random fashion.*

Step 5 ✎ To make the Log Cabin blocks, sew a 1-1/2-inch wide **DARK PRINT** strip to a 2-1/2-inch **DARK GOLD** center square; press. Press the seam allowance toward the strip just added. Trim the strip even with the edges of the center square.

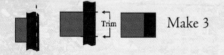

Make 3

Step 6 ✎ Turn the unit a quarter turn to the left. Sew another 1-1/2-inch wide **DARK PRINT** strip to the Step 5 unit; press and trim.

Step 7 ✎ Turn the unit a quarter turn to the left. Sew another 1-1/2-inch wide **DARK PRINT** strip to the Step 6 unit; press and trim.

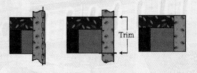

Step 8 ✎ Turn the unit a quarter turn to the left. Sew another 1-1/2-inch wide **DARK PRINT** strip to the Step 7 unit; press and trim.

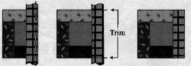

Step 9 ✎ Continue adding the remaining 1-1/2-inch wide **DARK PRINT** strips, referring to the Log Cabin block diagram for placement. Press and trim each strip before adding the next. After 3 strips have been added to all 4 sides of the center square, *each block should measure 8-1/2-inches square.*

Log Cabin Block

Make 3

Step 10 ☙ Sew the Log Cabin blocks and the remaining Step 3 flying geese units together; press. Sew this unit and the Step 4 unit together; press. *At this point the block should measure 12-1/2 x 32-1/2-inches.*

THIMBLEBERRIES VILLAGE Block 6

75

THIMBLEBERRIES® VILLAGE
BLOCK 7 - *Washington Ave. House*

CUTTING

From BROWN PRINT:
❋ Cut 3, 2-1/2 x 42-inch strips.
  From the strips cut:
    4, 2-1/2 x 16-1/2-inch rectangles
    8, 2-1/2 x 4-1/2-inch rectangles

From LIGHT GOLD PRINT:
❋ Cut 2, 4-1/2 x 6-1/2-inch rectangles
❋ Cut 3, 4-1/2-inch squares

From RED DIAGONAL PRINT:
❋ Cut 1, 4-1/2 x 8-1/2-inch rectangle

From BEIGE PRINT:
❋ Cut 1, 2-1/2 x 42-inch strip
❋ Cut 2, 6-1/2 x 8-1/2-inch rectangles

From GOLD/BLACK PLAID:
❋ Cut 1, 8-1/2 x 20-1/2-inch rectangle

From BROWN DIAGONAL PRINT:
❋ Cut 1, 2-1/2 x 42-inch strip.
  From the strip cut:
    1, 2-1/2 x 12-1/2-inch rectangle
    3, 2-1/2 x 8-1/2-inch rectangles

From GREEN/ROSE FLORAL:
❋ Cut 1, 2-1/2 x 42-inch strip.
  From the strip cut:
    2, 2-1/2 x 6-1/2-inch rectangles
    2, 2-1/2 x 4-1/2-inch rectangles

From RED PRINT :
❋ Cut 1, 2-1/2 x 42-inch strip

PIECING

Step 1 ✒ Sew 2-1/2 x 4-1/2-inch
  BROWN rectangles to the top and
  bottom edges of the 4-1/2-inch
  LIGHT GOLD squares; press. Sew the
  4-1/2 x 8-1/2-inch **RED DIAGONAL**
  PRINT rectangle to the bottom edge of
  this unit; press.

Make 3   Make 1

Step 2 ✒ Sew 2-1/2 x 4-1/2-inch
  BROWN rectangles to the bottom
  edge of the 4-1/2 x 6-1/2-inch **LIGHT**
  GOLD rectangles; press. Sew the
  units to the bottom edge of the
  remaining Step 1 units; press. Sew
  the 2-1/2 x 16-1/2-inch **BROWN**
  rectangles to both
  side edges of the
  units; press.

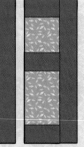

Make 2   Make 2

Step 3 ✎ Sew the Step 2 units to both side edges of the Step 1 unit; press. *At this point the house base should measure 16-1/2 x 20-1/2-inches.*

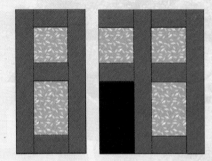

Make 1

Step 4 ✎ Sew 2-1/2 x 8-1/2-inch **BROWN DIAGONAL PRINT** rectangles to the 6-1/2 x 8-1/2-inch **BEIGE** rectangles; press.

Make 2

Step 5 ✎ Referring to the diagram, position the Step 4 units on the 8-1/2 x 20-1/2-inch **GOLD/BLACK PLAID** rectangle. Draw a diagonal line on each Step 5 unit; stitch, trim, and press. *At this point the roof should measure 8-1/2 x 20-1/2-inches.*

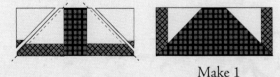

Make 1

Step 6 ✎ Sew the 2-1/2 x 6-1/2-inch **GREEN/ROSE FLORAL** rectangles to both side edges of the 2-1/2 x 8-1/2-inch **BROWN DIAGONAL PRINT** rectangle; press. Sew the 2-1/2 x 4-1/2-inch **GREEN/ROSE FLORAL** rectangles to both side edges of the 2-1/2 x 12-1/2-inch **BROWN DIAGONAL PRINT** rectangle; press. Sew these 2 units together; press. *At this point the steps unit should measure 4-1/2 x 28-1/2-inches.*

Make 1

(continued on the next page)

Step 7 ∾ Sew together the Step 5 roof, Step 3 house base, and Step 6 steps; press. *At this point the house unit should measure 20-1/2 x 28-1/2-inches.*

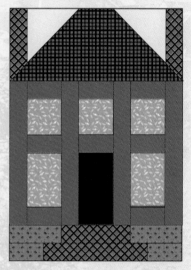

Step 8 ∾ Aligning long edges, sew the 2-1/2 x 42-inch **RED** and **BEIGE** strips together; press. Cut the strip set into segments. Sew the segments together, alternating colors; press. *At this point the checkerboard unit should measure 24-1/2 x 28-1/2-inches.*

Crosscut 14, 2-1/2-inch segments

Make 1

Step 9 ∾ Sew together the Step 7 house and the Step 8 checkerboard unit; press. *At this point the block should measure 24-1/2 x 28-1/2-inches.*

THIMBLEBERRIES VILLAGE Block 7

THIMBLEBERRIES® VILLAGE
BLOCK 8 - *Sunflower Garden*

CUTTING

From DARK GOLD PRINT:
❊ Cut 1, 2-7/8 x 20-inch strip.
  From the strip cut:
    6, 2-7/8-inch squares
❊ Cut 1, 2-1/2 x 42-inch strip.
  From the strip cut:
    12, 2-1/2-inch squares

From BEIGE PRINT:
❊ Cut 1, 2-7/8 x 42-inch strip.
  From the strip cut:
    8, 2-7/8-inch squares
❊ Cut 2, 2-1/2 x 42-inch strips.
  From the strips cut:
    3, 2-1/2 x 8-1/2-inch rectangles
    9, 2-1/2 x 4-1/2-inch rectangles
    3, 2-1/2-inch squares

From BLACK PRINT:
❊ Cut 3, 4-1/2-inch squares

From GREEN DIAGONAL PRINT:
❊ Cut 2, 2-7/8-inch squares
❊ Cut 1, 2-1/2 x 42-inch strip.
  From the strip cut:
    3, 2-1/2 x 6-1/2-inch rectangles
    3, 2-1/2 x 4-1/2-inch rectangles
    3, 2-1/2-inch squares

From RED FLORAL:
❊ Cut 1, 2-1/2 x 18-inch strip.
  From the strip cut:
    6, 2-1/2-inch squares

From GREEN/ROSE FLORAL:
❊ Cut 1, 2-1/2 x 18-inch strip.
  From the strip cut:
    6, 2-1/2-inch squares

PIECING

Step 1 ✒ To make the checkerboard unit, sew together the 2-1/2-inch **GREEN/ROSE FLORAL** squares and the 2-1/2-inch **RED FLORAL** squares; press.

Make 1

Step 2 ✒ Position a 2-1/2-inch **DARK GOLD** square on the corner of a 2-1/2 x 8-1/2-inch **BEIGE** rectangle. Draw a diagonal line on the square; stitch, trim, and press.

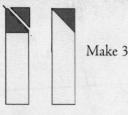

Make 3

79   *(continued on the next page)*

Step 3 ⤳ Position a 2-1/2-inch **DARK GOLD** square on the corner of a 2-1/2 x 4-1/2-inch **BEIGE** rectangle. Draw a diagonal line on the square; stitch, trim, and press.

 Make 3

Step 4 ⤳ With right sides together, layer 6, 2-7/8-inch **BEIGE** squares and 6, 2-7/8-inch **GOLD** squares in pairs. Press together, but do not sew. Cut the layered squares in half diagonally to make 12 sets of layered triangles. Stitch 1/4-inch from the diagonal edge of each pair of triangles; press.

Make 12, 2-1/2-inch triangle-pieced squares

Step 5 ⤳ With right sides together, layer 2, 2-7/8-inch **BEIGE** squares and 2, 2-7/8-inch **GREEN DIAGONAL PRINT** squares in pairs. Press together, but do not sew. Cut the layered squares in half diagonally to make 3 sets of layered triangles. Stitch 1/4-inch from the diagonal edge of the 3 pairs of triangles; press.

 Make 3, 2-1/2-inch triangle-pieced squares

Step 6 ⤳ Position a 2-1/2 x 4-1/2-inch **BEIGE** rectangle on the corner of a 2-1/2 x 4-1/2-inch **GREEN DIAGONAL PRINT** rectangle. Draw a diagonal line on the **BEIGE** rectangle; stitch, trim, and press.

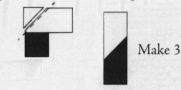 Make 3

Step 7 ⤳ Position a 2-1/2-inch **DARK GOLD** square on the corner of a 2-1/2 x 4-1/2-inch **BEIGE** rectangle. Draw a diagonal line on the square; stitch, trim, and press. Repeat this process at the opposite corner of the rectangle using a 2-1/2-inch **GREEN DIAGONAL PRINT** square.

 Make 3

Step 8 ⤳ Position a 2-1/2-inch **DARK GOLD** square on the corner of a 2-1/2 x 6-1/2-inch **GREEN DIAGONAL PRINT** rectangle. Draw a diagonal line on the square; stitch, trim, and press.

 Make 3

Step 9 ✒ Referring to the diagram, sew together the units to make one flower section. A flower section consists of:

- ❊ 1, 4-1/2-inch **BLACK** square
- ❊ 1, Step 2 unit
- ❊ 1, Step 3 unit
- ❊ 4, Step 4 triangle-pieced squares
- ❊ 1, Step 5 triangle-pieced square
- ❊ 1, Step 6 unit
- ❊ 1, Step 7 unit
- ❊ 1, Step 8 unit
- ❊ 1, 2-1/2-inch **BEIGE** square

Sew the flower section together in vertical rows; press. Sew the rows together; press. *At this point each flower section should measure 8-1/2 x 12-1/2-inches.*

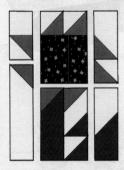

Make 3 flower sections

Step 10 ✒ Sew together the 3 flower sections; press. Sew the Step 1 checkerboard unit to the bottom edge of the flower unit; press. *At this point the block should measure 14-1/2 x 24-1/2-inches.*

THIMBLEBERRIES VILLAGE Block 8

THIMBLEBERRIES® VILLAGE
BLOCK 9 - *Summer Cottage*

CUTTING

From RED PRINT:
❋ Cut 1, 4-1/2 x 42-inch strip.
  From the strip cut:
    1, 4-1/2 x 8-1/2-inch rectangle
    2, 4-1/2-inch squares
    1, 2-1/2 x 8-1/2-inch rectangle
❋ Cut 1, 2-1/2 x 42-inch strip.
  From the strip cut:
    4, 2-1/2 x 6-1/2-inch rectangles
    4, 2-1/2-inch squares

From BEIGE PRINT:
❋ Cut 1, 4-1/2 x 42-inch strip.
  From the strip cut:
    2, 4-1/2 x 8-1/2-inch rectangles
    1, 2-1/2 x 12-inch strip
❋ Cut 2, 2-1/2 x 42-inch strips.
  From the strips cut:
    2, 2-1/2 x 8-1/2-inch rectangles
    6, 2-1/2 x 6-1/2-inch rectangles

From GOLD STAR PRINT:
❋ Cut 1, 2-1/2 x 42-inch strip.
  From the strip cut:
    3, 2-1/2 x 4-1/2-inch rectangles

From BROWN DIAGONAL PRINT:
❋ Cut 1, 4-1/2 x 42-inch strip.
  From the strip cut:
    1, 4-1/2 x 6-1/2-inch rectangle
    2, 2-1/2 x 8-1/2-inch rectangles

From CHESTNUT FLORAL:
❋ Cut 2, 4-1/2 x 6-1/2-inch rectangles

From MEDIUM BLUE PRINT:
❋ Cut 2, 8-1/2-inch squares
❋ Cut 2, 4-1/2-inch squares

From GREEN FLORAL:
❋ Cut 1, 4-1/2 x 6-1/2-inch rectangle
❋ Cut 1, 2-1/2 x 42-inch strip.
  From the strip cut:
    2, 2-1/2 x 12-inch strips
    6, 2-1/2-inch squares

PIECING

Step 1 ✒ Position a 4-1/2-inch **MEDIUM BLUE** square on the corner of the 4-1/2 x 8-1/2-inch **RED** rectangle. Draw a diagonal line on the square; stitch, trim, and press. Repeat this process at the opposite corner of the rectangle.

Make 1

Step 2 ✒ Sew 2 of the 2-1/2-inch **RED** squares to both side edges of a 2-1/2 x 4-1/2-inch **GOLD STAR PRINT** rectangle; press. Sew the 2-1/2 x 8-1/2-inch **RED** strip to the bottom edge of the unit; press. Sew the Step 1 unit to the top edge of the unit. *At this point the unit should measure 8-1/2-inches square.*

Make 1

Step 3 ✒ Position a 4-1/2-inch **RED** square on the corner of an 8-1/2-inch **MEDIUM BLUE** square. Draw a diagonal line on the **RED** square; stitch, trim, and press.

Make 1

Step 4 ✒ Sew a 2-1/2 x 8-1/2-inch **BEIGE** rectangle to the left edge of a 2-1/2 x 8-1/2-inch **BROWN DIAGONAL PRINT** rectangle. Sew a 4-1/2 x 8-1/2-inch **BEIGE** rectangle to the opposite edge of the **BROWN DIAGONAL PRINT** rectangle; press.

Make 2

(continued on the next page)

Step 5 ～ To make the chimney/roof units, layer the Step 4 units on top of the Step 3 units, notice the angles of the **RED** triangles, the position of the chimneys, and the stitching angles. Draw a diagonal line on the chimney unit, and stitch on the line. Trim away the excess corner fabric, leaving a 1/4-inch seam allowance; press.

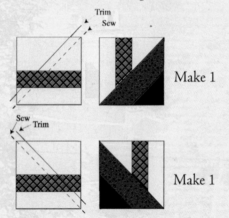

Make 1

Make 1

Step 6 ～ Sew the Step 5 units to both side edges of the Step 2 unit; press. *At this point the unit should measure 8-1/2 x 24-1/2-inches.*

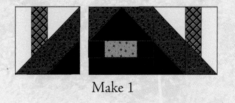

Make 1

Step 7 ～ Sew a 2-1/2-inch **RED** square to a 2-1/2 x 4-1/2-inch **GOLD STAR PRINT** rectangle; press. Sew 2-1/2 x 6-1/2-inch **RED** rectangles to both side edges of the unit; press. Make 2 window units. Sew these units to both side edges of the 4-1/2 x 6-1/2-inch **BROWN DIAGONAL PRINT** rectangle; press. Sew 4-1/2 x 6-1/2-inch **CHESTNUT FLORAL** rectangles to both side edges of this unit; press. *At this point the unit should measure 6-1/2 x 24-1/2-inches.*

Make 1

Step 8 ～ Position a 2-1/2-inch **GREEN FLORAL** square on the corner of a 2-1/2 x 6-1/2-inch **BEIGE** rectangle. Draw a diagonal line on the square; stitch, trim, and press. Notice the 2 different angles of the stitching lines.

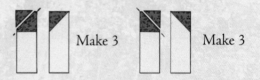

Make 3   Make 3

Step 9 ✎ Aligning long edges, sew a 2-1/2 x 12-inch **GREEN FLORAL** strip to both side edges of a 2-1/2 x 12-inch **BEIGE** strip, and cut into segments.

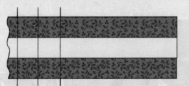

Crosscut 4, 2-1/2-inch wide segments

Step 10 ✎ Sew together the Step 8 units, Step 9 segments, and the 4-1/2 x 6-1/2-inch **GREEN FLORAL** rectangle; press. *At this point the unit should measure 6-1/2 x 24-1/2-inches.*

Make 1

Step 11 ✎ Sew together the units from Step 6, Step 7, and Step 10; press. *At this point the block should measure 20-1/2 x 24-1/2-inches.*

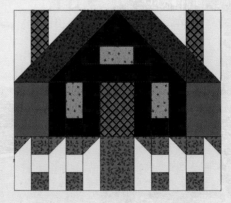

THIMBLEBERRIES VILLAGE Block 9

THIMBLEBERRIES® VILLAGE
BLOCK 10 - *Blossom Time*

CUTTING

From BROWN DIAGONAL PRINT:
❋ Cut 1, 2-1/2 x 24-inch strip

From BEIGE PRINT:
❋ Cut 4, 2-1/2 x 42-inch strips.
   From the strips cut:
     1, 2-1/2 x 24-inch strip
     8, 2-1/2 x 6-1/2-inch rectangles
     32, 2-1/2-inch squares
❋ Cut 1, 1-1/2 x 42-inch strip.
   From the strip cut:
     24, 1-1/2-inch squares

From each GOLD PRINT, BLUE FLORAL, RED FLORAL, and PURPLE PRINT:
❋ Cut 2, 4-1/2-inch squares

From GREEN FLORAL:
❋ Cut 2, 2-1/2 x 42-inch strips.
   From the strips cut:
     10, 2-1/2 x 4-1/2-inch rectangles
     5, 2-1/2-inch squares

From GREEN/ROSE FLORAL:
❋ Cut 1, 2-1/2 x 42-inch strip.
   From the strip cut:
     6, 2-1/2 x 4-1/2-inch rectangles
     3, 2-1/2-inch squares

PIECING

Step 1 ❧ Aligning the long edges, sew together the 2-1/2 x 24-inch **BROWN DIAGONAL PRINT** and **BEIGE** strips; press. Cut the strip set into segments.

Crosscut 9, 2-1/2-inch wide segments

Step 2 ❧ Sew the segments together in 3 horizontal rows, alternating colors; press. Sew the rows together; press. *At this point the checkerboard unit should measure 6-1/2 x 12-1/2-inches.*

Make 1

Step 3 ❧ Position 1-1/2-inch **BEIGE** squares on 3 corners of each 4-1/2-inch **GOLD, BLUE, RED,** and **PURPLE** square. Draw a diagonal line on the **BEIGE** squares; stitch, trim, and press.

Make 2 from each color (8 total)

Step 4 ✍ To make the **GREEN FLORAL** right leaf units, position a 2-1/2-inch **BEIGE** square on the corner of a 2-1/2 x 4-1/2-inch **GREEN FLORAL** rectangle. Draw a diagonal line on the square; stitch, trim, and press. Notice the direction of the stitching line. Repeat this process at the opposite corner of the rectangle. Repeat this process to make the **GREEN/ROSE FLORAL** right leaf units.

Make 5 **GREEN FLORAL**
right leaf units
Make 3 **GREEN/ROSE FLORAL**
right leaf units

Step 5 ✍ To make the **GREEN FLORAL** and **GREEN/ROSE FLORAL** left leaf units, refer to Step 4. Notice the change in the direction of the stitching line.

Make 5 **GREEN FLORAL**
left leaf units
Make 3 **GREEN/ROSE FLORAL**
left leaf units

Step 6 ✍ Sew a 2-1/2-inch coordinating **GREEN** square to the right edge of the Step 5 left leaf units; press.

Make 5 **GREEN FLORAL**
Make 3 **GREEN/ROSE FLORAL**

(continued on the next page)

Step 7 ↪ Sew the Step 4 right leaf units to the Step 3 flowers; press. Sew the Step 6 left leaf units to the bottom edge of the flowers; press. *At this point the flower units should measure 6-1/2-inches square.*

Make 5 GREEN FLORAL
Make 3 GREEN/ROSE FLORAL

Step 8 ↪ Referring to the block diagram, sew together the Step 7 flowers and the 2-1/2 x 6-1/2-inch **BEIGE** rectangles in 2 vertical rows; press. Sew the vertical rows together; press. Add the Step 2 checkerboard unit to the bottom edge; press. *At this point the block should measure 12-1/2 x 38-1/2-inches.*

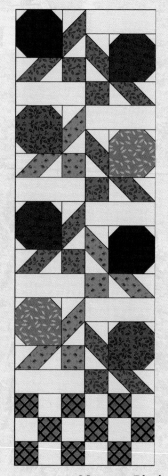

THIMBLEBERRIES VILLAGE Block 10

THIMBLEBERRIES® VILLAGE
BLOCK II - *Lakeside*

CUTTING

From RED PRINT:
❋ Cut 2, 2-1/2 x 42-inch strips.
From the strips cut:
    3, 2-1/2 x 16-inch strips

From BEIGE PRINT:
❋ Cut 2, 2-7/8 x 42-inch strips
❋ Cut 1, 8-7/8 x 42-inch strip.
From the strip cut:
    1, 8-7/8-inch square
    3, 2-1/2 x 16-inch strips

From BLUE FLORAL:
❋ Cut 1, 2-7/8 x 42-inch strip
❋ Cut 1, 8-7/8-inch square

From DARK BLUE PRINT:
❋ Cut 1, 2-7/8 x 42-inch strip
❋ Cut 1, 8-7/8-inch square

PIECING

Step 1 ✍ Aligning long edges, sew 2-1/2 x 16-inch **RED** strips to the top and bottom edges of 1 of the 2-1/2 x 16-inch **BEIGE** strips; press. Cut the strip set into segments.

Crosscut 6, 2-1/2-inch wide segments

Step 2 ✍ Aligning long edges, sew 2-1/2 x 16-inch **BEIGE** strips to the top and bottom edges of 1 of the 2-1/2 x 16-inch **RED** strips; press. Cut the strip set into segments.

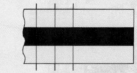

Crosscut 6, 2-1/2-inch wide segments

Step 3 ✍ Sew the Step 1 and Step 2 segments together as diagramed; press. *At this point the checkerboard unit should measure 6-1/2 x 24-1/2-inches.*

Make 1

(continued on the next page)

Step 4 ✒ Cut the 8-7/8-inch **BEIGE,
BLUE FLORAL,** and **DARK BLUE**
squares in half diagonally. You will be
using only one of the **BLUE FLORAL**
triangles, and one of the **DARK BLUE**
triangles.

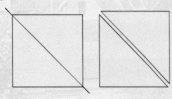

Step 5 ✒ Sew a **BEIGE** triangle and a
BLUE FLORAL triangle together;
press.

Make 1, 8-1/2-inch
triangle-pieced square

Step 6 ✒ With right sides together,
layer together the 2-7/8 x 42-inch
BLUE FLORAL strip and 1 of the
2-7/8 x 42-inch **BEIGE** strips. Press
together, but do not sew. Cut the layered
strip into squares. Cut the layered
squares in half diagonally to make 20

sets of layered triangles. Stitch 1/4-inch
from the diagonal edge of each pair of
triangles; press.

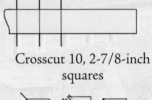

Crosscut 10, 2-7/8-inch
squares

Make 20, 2-1/2-inch
triangle-pieced squares

Step 7 ✒ Sew together 4 pairs
of Step 6 triangle-pieced
squares; press. Sew the pairs
together in a strip; press. *At
this point the unit should measure
4-1/2 x 8-1/2-inches.*
Make 1

Step 8 ✒ Sew together 6 pairs of Step 6
triangle-pieced squares; press. Sew the
pairs together in a strip; press.
*At this point the unit should measure
4-1/2 x 12-1/2-inches.*

Make 1

Step 9 ✒ Sew the Step 7 strip to the right edge of the Step 5 triangle-pieced square; press. Sew the Step 8 strip to the top edge of this unit; press. *At this point the block should measure 12-1/2-inches square.*

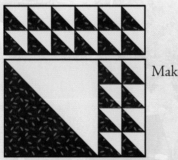

Make 1

Step 10 ✒ To make another pieced block, repeat Steps 5 through 9 using the **BEIGE** fabric and the **DARK BLUE** fabric. *At this point the block should measure 12-1/2-inches square.*

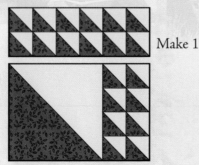

Make 1

Step 11 ✒ Sew the Step 9 and Step 10 blocks together; press. Sew the Step 3 checkerboard unit to the top edge of the blocks; press. *At this point the block should measure 18-1/2 x 24-1/2-inches.*

THIMBLEBERRIES VILLAGE Block 11

THIMBLEBERRIES® VILLAGE
BLOCK 12 - *Potting Shed*

CUTTING

From GOLD/BLACK PLAID:
❋ Cut 1, 6-1/2 x 12-1/2-inch rectangle

From BEIGE PRINT:
❋ Cut 1, 6-1/2 x 42-inch strip.
  From the strip cut:
      2, 6-1/2-inch squares
      1, 4-7/8-inch square
      1, 2-7/8-inch square
      2, 2-1/2 x 3-1/2-inch rectangles
❋ Cut 1, 2-1/2 x 42-inch strip.
  From the strip cut:
      4, 2-1/2 x 4-1/2-inch rectangles
      8, 2-1/2-inch squares

From RED DIAGONAL PRINT:
❋ Cut 1, 4-1/2 x 42-inch strip.
  From the strip cut:
      2, 4-1/2 x 6-1/2-inch rectangles
      2, 1-1/2-inch squares

From BROWN DIAGONAL PRINT:
❋ Cut 1, 4-1/2 x 6-1/2-inch rectangle

From GREEN TREE PRINT:
❋ Cut 1, 4-7/8 x 42-inch strip.
  From the strip cut:
      1, 4-7/8-inch square
      1, 2-7/8-inch square
      1, 2-1/2 x 10-1/2-inch rectangle
      3, 2-1/2 x 4-1/2-inch rectangles
      3, 2-1/2-inch squares

From GOLD PRINT:
❋ Cut 2, 2-1/2 x 20-inch strips.
  From the strips cut:
      2, 2-1/2 x 6-1/2-inch rectangles
      4, 2-1/2-inch squares

From CHESTNUT FLORAL:
❋ Cut 1, 2-1/2-inch square

PIECING

Step 1 ✎ Position a 6-1/2-inch **BEIGE** square on the corner of the 6-1/2 x 12-1/2-inch **GOLD/BLACK PLAID** rectangle. Draw a diagonal line on the square; stitch, trim, and press. Repeat this process at the opposite corner of the rectangle.

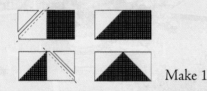

Make 1

Step 2 ✎ Position 1-1/2-inch **RED DIAGONAL PRINT** squares on 2 adjacent corners of the 4-1/2 x 6-1/2-inch **BROWN DIAGONAL PRINT** rectangle; press. Draw a diagonal line on the squares; stitch, trim, and press. Sew the 4-1/2 x 6-1/2-inch **RED DIAGONAL PRINT** rectangles to the side edges of the door unit; press.

Make 1   Make 1

Step 3 ✎ Sew the Step 1 roof unit to the top edge of the Step 2 door unit; press. *At this point the unit should measure 12-1/2-inches square.*

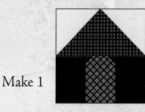

Make 1

Step 4 ✎ With right sides together, layer the 4-7/8-inch **GREEN TREE PRINT** and **BEIGE** squares. Press together, but do not sew. Cut the layered square in half diagonally. Stitch 1/4-inch from the diagonal edge of 1 pair of triangles; press. *At this point the triangle-pieced square should measure 4-1/2-inches square.*

Make 1, 4-1/2-inch triangle-pieced square

Step 5 ✎ Repeat Step 4 using 2-7/8-inch **GREEN TREE PRINT** and **BEIGE** squares. Cut, stitch, trim, and press. You will be using only 1 triangle-pieced square. *At this point the triangle-pieced square should measure 2-1/2-inches square.*

Make 1, 2-1/2-inch triangle-pieced square

(continued on the next page)

Step 6 ✏ Position a 2-1/2-inch **BEIGE** square on the corner of a 2-1/2 x 4-1/2-inch **GREEN TREE PRINT** rectangle. Draw a diagonal line on the square; stitch, trim, and press.

 Make 3

Step 7 ✏ Referring to the Step 8 diagram, sew the Step 6 units together, add the Step 4 unit to the top edge; press.

Step 8 ✏ Position a 2-1/2-inch **BEIGE** square on the corner of the 2-1/2 x 10-1/2-inch **GREEN TREE PRINT** rectangle. Draw a diagonal line on the square; stitch, trim, and press. Sew this unit to the left edge of the Step 7 unit; press. *At this point the unit should measure 6-1/2 x 10-1/2-inches.*

Make 1   Make 1

Step 9 ✏ Position a 2-1/2-inch **BEIGE** square on the left corner of a 2-1/2 x 6-1/2-inch **GOLD** rectangle. Position a 2-1/2-inch **GREEN TREE PRINT** square on the right corner of

the rectangle. Draw diagonal lines on the squares; stitch, trim, and press. *At this point each unit should measure 2-1/2 x 6-1/2-inches.*

  Make 2

Step 10 ✏ Position a 2-1/2-inch **GOLD** square on the corner of a 2-1/2 x 4-1/2-inch **BEIGE** rectangle. Draw a diagonal line on the square; stitch, trim, and press. Make 3 of these units. Sew a 2-1/2-inch **BEIGE** square to 1 unit. Sew the Step 5 triangle-pieced square to another unit. The remaining unit will be sewn to the trunk unit in Step 12.

Make 3   Make 1   Make 1

Step 11 ✏ Position a 2-1/2-inch **GOLD** square on the corner of a 2-1/2 x 4-1/2-inch **BEIGE** rectangle. Draw a diagonal line on the square; stitch, trim, and press. Repeat this process at the opposite corner of the rectangle using a 2-1/2-inch **GREEN TREE PRINT** square. Sew a 2-1/2-inch **BEIGE** square to the left edge of this unit; press.

Make 1   Make 1

Step 12 ✌ Sew the 2-1/2 x 3-1/2-inch **BEIGE** rectangles to both side edges of the 2-1/2-inch **CHESTNUT FLORAL** square; press. Sew this unit to the right edge of the remaining Step 10 unit. *At this point the unit should measure 2-1/2 x 12-1/2-inches.*

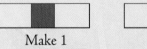

Make 1

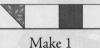

Make 1

Step 13 ✌ Referring to the diagram, sew together the Step 9, Step 10, and Step 11 units; press. Sew the Step 8 unit to the right edge of this unit; press. Sew the Step 12 unit to the bottom edge of the unit; press. *At this point the unit should measure 12-1/2-inches square.*

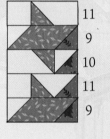

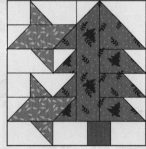

11
9
10
11
9

Step 14 ✌ Sew together the Step 3 unit and the Step 13 unit; press. *At this point the block should measure 12-1/2 x 24-1/2-inches.*

THIMBLEBERRIES VILLAGE Block 12

FINISHING THE QUILT

QUILT CENTER

QUILT CENTER ASSEMBLY

Referring to the quilt assembly diagram for block placement, lay out the 12 blocks in sections. Sew the blocks together in sections; press. Sew the sections together; press.

QUILT ASSEMBLY DIAGRAM

BORDERS

NOTE: *The yardage given allows for the border strips to be cut on the crosswise grain. Diagonally piece the strips as needed, referring to* **Diagonal Piecing** *instructions on page 253. Read through* **Border** *instructions on page 250, for general instructions on adding borders.*

CUTTING

From BEIGE PRINT:
❋ Cut 8, 2-1/2 x 42-inch inner border strips

From RED PRINT:
❋ Cut 9, 2-1/2 x 42-inch first middle border strips

From BLACK PRINT:
❋ Cut 9, 1-1/2 x 42-inch second middle border strips

From GREEN FLORAL:
❋ Cut 10, 5-1/2 x 42-inch outer border strips

Attaching the Borders

Step 1 ❧ Attach the 2-1/2-inch wide **BEIGE** inner border strips.

Step 2 ❧ Attach the 2-1/2-inch wide **RED** first middle border strips.

Step 3 ❧ Attach the 1-1/2-inch wide **BLACK** second middle border strips.

Step 4 ❧ Attach the 5-1/2-inch wide **GREEN FLORAL** outer border strips.

Putting It All Together

❋ Cut the 7 yard length of backing fabric in half crosswise to make 3, 2-1/3 yard lengths. Refer to **Quilting the Project** on page 252 for complete instructions.

Binding

From BROWN DIAGONAL PRINT:
❋ Cut 10, 2-3/4 x 42-inch strips

Sew the binding to the quilt using a 3/8-inch seam allowance. This measurement will produce a 1/2-inch wide finished binding. Refer to **Binding** and **Diagonal Piecing** on page 253 for complete instructions.

SAFE HAVEN™

Images of safety and rest for winged creatures bring home a message of love and refuge for all.

*Q*uilts are a terrific way to decorate a home. They communicate messages of love, warmth and caring. SAFE HAVEN epitomizes these feelings that a quilt can evoke. Celebrating the folk art traditions of birdhouses, the blocks of SAFE HAVEN depict a variety of birdhouses that collectively communicate the message of love and home. This quilt is a "strippy"—in other words, everything on the quilt runs vertically.

This quilt stirs memories of a bygone era. It is traditional in its design, and harkens back to the early 1800s. Perhaps as a child one of your first woodworking projects was a birdhouse, and making this quilt will transport you back to your childhood days.

SAFE HAVEN

88 x 96 inches

Fabrics & Supplies

2-7/8 yards
BEIGE PRINT
for all 12 blocks

1/4 yard
CORAL PLAID
for blocks 1, 4

1/4 yard
MEDIUM GREEN PRINT
for blocks 1, 8, 9, 11, 12

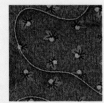

6" square
ORANGE PRINT
for block 1

2/3 yard
RED PRINT #1
for blocks 1, 3, 7, 10, 12

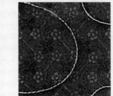

1/2 yard
DARK BLUE PRINT
for blocks 1, 3, 9, 12

1/2 yard
BLUE PRINT #1
for blocks 1, 7, 8, 9

3/8 yard
LIGHT GOLD PRINT
for blocks 1, 3, 6, 8, 10

5/8 yard
BROWN PRINT #1
for blocks 1, 3, 7, 8, 9, 12

2/3 yard
LIGHT GREEN PRINT
for blocks 2, 4, 5, 6, 7

1/4 yard
BROWN PLAID
for blocks 3, 7, 10

1 yard
DARK GREEN PRINT
for blocks 2, 4, 5, 6, 7, 9, 11, 12

1/2 yard
BLUE PRINT #2
for blocks 3, 5, 8, 10

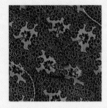

3/8 yard
BROWN PRINT #2
for blocks 2, 3, 10

1/2 yard
GOLD PRINT #2
for blocks 3, 7, 8, 9, 11

1/3 yard
RED PLAID
for blocks 2, 7, 8

6" x 18" piece
BRICK PRINT #1
for blocks 4, 5

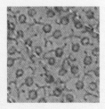

3/4 yard **GOLD PRINT #1**
for blocks 2, 7, 8, 12,
first middle border

1-1/4 yards
EGGPLANT PRINT
for blocks 4, 5, 7, 11,
narrow lattice, inner border

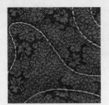

1/2 yard
RED PRINT #2
for blocks 4, 6, 7, 9, 11

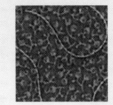

5/8 yard
BRICK PRINT #2
for block 11,
second middle border

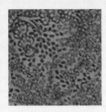

4" x 12" piece
PLUM PRINT #1
block 6

2-1/2 yards
**LARGE GOLD
FLORAL**
for wide lattice, outer border

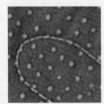

1/8 yard
PLUM PRINT #2
for blocks 6, 11

7/8 yard
**BLUE DIAGONAL
CHECK**
for binding

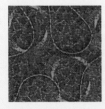

1/2 yard
ROSE PRINT
for blocks 6, 9, 12

8 yards backing fabric
quilt batting, at least
92 x 100-inches

Before beginning this project, read through **Getting Started** on page 244.

*This fabric key should be used as a helpful guideline in selecting fabric for your quilt project.
We cannot guarantee that a specific fabric will be available at your favorite quilt store,
but suitable substitutions can be found.*

SAFE HAVEN
BLOCK - *One*

CUTTING

From BEIGE PRINT:
✳ Cut 1, 4-7/8 x 42-inch strip.
   From the strip cut:
      6, 4-7/8-inch squares
✳ Cut 1, 2-7/8 x 42-inch strip

From CORAL PLAID, MEDIUM GREEN PRINT, ORANGE PRINT, and DARK BLUE PRINT:
✳ Cut 1, 4-7/8-inch square from each fabric

From RED PRINT #1:
✳ Cut 1, 4-7/8 x 22-inch strip.
   From the strip cut:
      1, 4-7/8-inch square
      1, 4-1/2 x 8-1/2-inch rectangle
      1, 4-1/2 x 6-1/2-inch rectangle

From BLUE PRINT #1:
✳ Cut 1, 4-7/8 x 42-inch strip.
   From the strip cut:
      1, 4-7/8-inch square
      2, 2-1/2 x 7-1/2-inch rectangles
      4, 2-1/2-inch squares
      1, 1-1/2 x 4-1/2-inch rectangle
      2, 1-1/2-inch squares

From LIGHT GOLD PRINT:
✳ Cut 1, 3-1/2 x 17-inch strip.
   From the strip cut:
      2, 3-1/2-inch squares
      1, 1-1/2 x 8-1/2-inch rectangle

From BROWN PRINT #1:
✳ Cut 1, 2-7/8 x 42-inch strip

Piecing

Step 1 ✦ With right sides together, layer the 4-7/8-inch **CORAL PLAID** square with a 4-7/8-inch **BEIGE** square. Cut the layered square in half diagonally to make 2 sets of layered triangles. Stitch 1/4-inch from the diagonal edge of each pair of triangles; press. *At this point each triangle-pieced square should measure 4-1/2-inches square.* Repeat this process using the 4-7/8-inch **MEDIUM GREEN, ORANGE, RED #1,** and **DARK BLUE** squares with the 4-7/8-inch **BEIGE** squares.

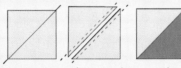

Make 2, 4-1/2-inch triangle-pieced squares
using each fabric

Step 2 ✦ Sew the triangle-pieced squares together in pairs to make 5 flying geese units; press. *At this point each flying geese unit should measure 4-1/2 x 8-1/2-inches.*

Make a total of 5 flying geese units

Step 3 ✦ Referring to the block diagram, sew the flying geese units together; press. *At this point the flying geese section should measure 8-1/2 x 20-1/2-inches.*

Step 4 ✦ As in Step 1, layer a 4-7/8-inch **BLUE #1** square with a 4-7/8-inch **BEIGE** square. Cut the layered square in half diagonally; stitch and press. Position a 3-1/2-inch **LIGHT GOLD** square on the **BLUE #1** side of each triangle-pieced square. Draw a diagonal line on the **LIGHT GOLD** square; stitch on the line. Trim the seam allowance to 1/4-inch; press. Make 2 units. Sew the triangle-pieced squares together to make the roof unit; press. *At this point the roof unit should measure 4-1/2 x 8-1/2-inches.*

Make 2, 4-1/2-inch   Make 2   Make 1
triangle-pieced
squares

(continued on the next page)

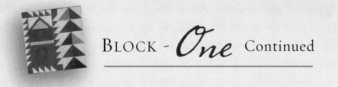
Step 5 ❧ Sew the 4-1/2 x 8-1/2-inch **RED #1** rectangle to the bottom edge of the roof section; press. Sew the 1-1/2 x 8-1/2-inch **LIGHT GOLD** rectangle to the bottom edge of the unit; press. *At this point the upper house unit should measure 8-1/2 x 9-1/2-inches.*

Make 1

Step 6 ❧ With right sides together, position the 1-1/2-inch **BLUE #1** squares on the upper corners of the 4-1/2 x 6-1/2-inch **RED #1** rectangle. Draw a diagonal line on the **BLUE #1** squares; stitch, trim, and press. Sew the 1-1/2 x 4-1/2-inch **BLUE #1** rectangle to the top edge of this unit; press. Sew the 2-1/2 x 7-1/2-inch **BLUE #1** rectangles to both side edges of the unit; press. *At this point the lower house unit should measure 7-1/2 x 8-1/2-inches.*

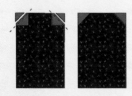

Make 1

Step 7 ❧ Referring to the block diagram, sew the Step 6 lower house unit to the Step 5 upper house unit; press. *At this point the house unit should measure 8-1/2 x 16-1/2-inches.*

Step 8 ❧ With right sides together, layer together the 2-7/8 x 42-inch **BROWN #1** and **BEIGE** strips. Press together, but do not sew. Cut the layered strip into 12, 2-7/8-inch squares. Cut each layered square in half diagonally to make 24 sets of layered triangles. Stitch 1/4-inch from the diagonal edge of each pair of triangles; press. *At this point each triangle-pieced square should measure 2-1/2-inches square.*

Crosscut 12,
2-7/8-inch squares

Make 24, 2-1/2-inch
triangle-pieced squares

Step 9 ❧ Referring to the block diagram, sew 4 triangle-pieced squares together for the top sawtooth section; press. Repeat this process to make a sawtooth section for the bottom of the house unit; press. Sew these sections to the house unit; press.

 Make 2

Step 10 ❧ Referring to the block diagram, sew 8 triangle-pieced squares together for each side sawtooth section; press. Sew 2-1/2-inch **BLUE #1** squares to both ends of the sawtooth sections; press. Sew these sections to the side edges of the house unit; press.

Step 11 ❧ Referring to the block diagram, sew the Step 3 flying geese section to the right edge of the Step 10 house/sawtooth unit; press. *At this point the block should measure 20-1/2 inches square.* Refer to **Appliqué the Birdhouse Holes** on page 150 for complete instructions on adding the birdhouse holes.

SAFE HAVEN Block 1

Safe Haven
Block - *Two*

Cutting

From BEIGE PRINT:
❀ Cut 1, 6-7/8 x 42-inch strip.
   From the strip cut:
      1, 6-7/8-inch square
      8, 2-1/2-inch squares
      2, 1-1/2 x 5-1/2-inch rectangles
❀ Cut 1, 2-1/2 x 42-inch strip.
   From the strip cut:
      16, 2-1/2-inch squares

From LIGHT GREEN PRINT:
❀ Cut 1, 6-1/4-inch square. Cut the
   square diagonally into quarters, to make
   4 triangles. You will be using
   only 2 triangles.
❀ Cut 1, 5-7/8-inch square

From DARK GREEN PRINT:
❀ Cut 1, 6-1/4 x 42-inch strip.
   From the strip cut:
      1, 6-1/4-inch square. Cut the square
      diagonally into quarters, to make
      4 triangles. You will be using only
      2 triangles.
      1, 5-7/8-inch square
      2, 2-1/2 x 16-1/2-inch strips
❀ Cut 1, 2-1/2 x 42-inch strip.
   From the strip cut:
      2, 2-1/2 x 16-1/2-inch strips

From BROWN PRINT #2:
❀ Cut 1, 6-7/8-inch square
❀ Cut 4, 2-1/2-inch squares
❀ Cut 1, 1-1/2 x 12-1/2-inch rectangle

From RED PLAID:
❀ Cut 1, 5-7/8-inch square. Cut the
   square in half diagonally, to make
   2 triangles.
❀ Cut 4, 2-1/2-inch squares

From GOLD PRINT #1:
❀ Cut 2, 2-1/2 x 42-inch strips.
   From the strips cut:
      12, 2-1/2 x 4-1/2-inch rectangles

Piecing

Step 1 ❧ With right sides together, layer the 5-7/8-inch **LIGHT GREEN** and **DARK GREEN** squares. Cut the layered square in half diagonally to make 2 sets of layered triangles. Stitch 1/4-inch from the diagonal edge of each pair of triangles to make 2 triangle-pieced squares; press. *At this point each triangle-pieced square should measure 5-1/2-inches square.*

Make 2, 5-1/2-inch triangle-pieced squares

Step 2 ✒ With right sides together, layer the 6-7/8-inch **BROWN #2** square with the 6-7/8-inch **BEIGE** square. Cut the layered square in half diagonally to make 2 sets of layered triangles. Stitch 1/4-inch from the diagonal edge of each pair of triangles to make 2 triangle-pieced squares; press. *At this point each triangle-pieced square should measure 6-1/2-inches square.*

Make 2, 6-1/2-inch triangle-pieced squares

Step 3 ✒ With right sides together, position a Step 1 triangle-pieced square on the **BROWN #2** side of each Step 2 triangle-pieced square. Draw a diagonal line on the pieced square; stitch, trim, and press. Make 2 units. Sew the pieced squares together to make the roof section; press. *At this point the roof section should measure 6-1/2 x 12-1/2-inches.*

Make 2   Make 1

Step 4 ✒ Layer a **LIGHT GREEN** triangle on a **DARK GREEN** triangle. Stitch along the bias edge; press. Repeat with the remaining **LIGHT GREEN** and **DARK GREEN** triangle, stitching along the same bias edge of each triangle set.

Bias edges

   Make 2

Step 5 ✒ Sew together a Step 4 triangle unit and a **RED PLAID** triangle; press. Make 2 units. Sew the pieced squares together; press. Sew 1-1/2 x 5-1/2-inch **BEIGE** rectangles to both side edges of the unit; press. *At this point the house section should measure 5-1/2 x 12-1/2-inches.*

Make 2   Make 1

(continued on the next page)

Step 6 ✒ Sew the Step 3 roof section to the top edge of the Step 5 house section; press. Sew the 1-1/2 x 12-1/2-inch **BROWN #2** rectangle to the bottom edge of the section; press. *At this point the house unit should measure 12-1/2-inches square.*

Make 1

Step 7 ✒ With right sides together, position a 2-1/2-inch **BEIGE** square on the corner of a 2-1/2 x 4-1/2-inch **GOLD #1** rectangle. Draw a diagonal line on the square; stitch, trim, and press. Repeat this process at the opposite corner of the rectangle. Make 12 units. Sew together 3 units; press. Make 4 flying geese strips. *At this point each flying geese strip should measure 2-1/2 x 12-1/2-inches.*

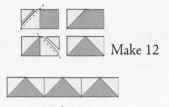

Make 12

Make 4

Step 8 ✒ Referring to the block diagram, sew the Step 7 flying geese strips to the top/bottom edges of the Step 6 house unit; press. Sew 2-1/2-inch **BROWN #2** squares to the remaining Step 7 flying geese strips; press. Sew the units to the side edges of the house unit; press. *At this point the block should measure 16-1/2-inches square.*

Step 9 ✒ Sew 2-1/2 x 16-1/2-inch **DARK GREEN** strips to the top/bottom edges of the Step 8 block; press. Sew 2-1/2-inch **RED PLAID** squares to the remaining **DARK GREEN** strips; press. Sew these units to the side edges of the block; press. *At this point the block should measure 20-1/2-inches square.* Refer to **Appliqué the Birdhouse Holes** on page 150 for complete instructions on adding the birdhouse hole.

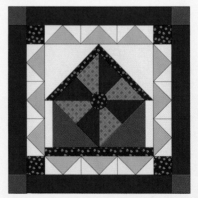

SAFE HAVEN Block 2

SAFE HAVEN
BLOCK - *Three*

CUTTING

From BEIGE PRINT:
❋ Cut 1, 4-1/2 x 42-inch strip.
   From the strip cut:
      6, 4-1/2-inch squares
      2, 3-1/2-inch squares
❋ Cut 2, 2-1/2 x 42-inch strips.
   From the strips cut:
      28, 2-1/2-inch squares

From DARK BLUE PRINT:
❋ Cut 1, 4-1/2 x 26-inch strip.
   From the strip cut:
      2, 4-1/2 x 8-1/2-inch rectangles
      3, 2-1/2 x 4-1/2-inch rectangles

From BROWN PRINT #1:
❋ Cut 1, 2-1/2 x 42-inch strip.
   From the strip cut:
      2, 2-1/2 x 6-1/2-inch rectangles
      3, 2-1/2 x 4-1/2-inch rectangles
      1, 2-1/2 x 3-1/2-inch rectangle
      4, 2-1/2-inch squares
❋ Cut 1, 1-1/2 x 16-inch strip.
   From the strip cut:
      1, 1-1/2 x 4-1/2-inch rectangle
      1, 1-1/2 x 6-1/2-inch rectangle
      2, 1-1/2-inch squares

From BROWN PLAID:
❋ Cut 1, 4-1/2 x 6-1/2-inch rectangle

From RED PRINT #1:
❋ Cut 1, 4-1/2 x 42-inch strip.
   From the strip cut:
      1, 4-1/2 x 6-1/2-inch rectangle
      2, 2-1/2 x 6-1/2-inch rectangles
      2, 2-1/2 x 4-1/2-inch rectangles
      4, 2-1/2-inch squares

From LIGHT GOLD PRINT:
❋ Cut 1, 4-1/2 x 6-1/2-inch rectangle

From BLUE PRINT #2:
❋ Cut 1, 4-1/2 x 8-1/2-inch rectangle
❋ Cut 1, 1-1/2 x 8-1/2-inch rectangle

From GOLD PRINT #2:
❋ Cut 1, 2-1/2 x 42-inch strip.
   From the strip cut:
      2, 2-1/2 x 7-1/2-inch rectangles
      3, 2-1/2 x 4-1/2-inch rectangles
      4, 2-1/2-inch squares
      2, 1-1/2-inch squares

From BROWN PRINT #2:
❋ Cut 3, 2-1/2 x 4-1/2-inch rectangles

PIECING

Step 1 ❧ With right sides together, position a 4-1/2-inch **BEIGE** square on the corner of a 4-1/2 x 8-1/2-inch **DARK BLUE** rectangle. Draw a diagonal line on the square; stitch, trim, and press. Repeat this process at the opposite corner of the rectangle. *At this point each roof unit should measure 4-1/2 x 8-1/2-inches.*

Make 2

Step 2 ❧ Repeat Step 1 using 4-1/2-inch **BEIGE** squares and the 4-1/2 x 8-1/2-inch **BLUE #2** rectangle. Make 1 roof unit.

Step 3 ❧ With right sides together, position 2-1/2-inch **BROWN #1** squares on opposite corners of the 4-1/2 x 6-1/2-inch **BROWN PLAID** rectangle. Draw a diagonal line on the squares; stitch, trim, and press. Repeat this process at the opposite corners of the rectangle. Sew 2-1/2 x 6-1/2-inch **BROWN #1** rectangles to both side edges of this unit; press. Sew a Step 1

roof unit to the top edge of the house base; press. *At this point the house unit should measure 8-1/2 x 10-1/2-inches.*

Make 1   Make 1

Step 4 ❧ Repeat Step 3 using 2-1/2-inch **RED #1** squares and the 4-1/2 x 6-1/2-inch **LIGHT GOLD** rectangle. Sew 2-1/2 x 6-1/2-inch **RED #1** rectangles to both side edges of the unit; press. Sew a Step 1 roof unit to the top edge of the house base; press.

(continued on the next page)

113

BLOCK - *Three* Continued

Step 5 ✏ Repeat Step 3 using 2-1/2-inch **GOLD #2** squares and the 4-1/2 x 6-1/2-inch **RED #1** rectangle. Sew the 1-1/2 x 4-1/2-inch **BROWN #1** rectangle to the bottom edge of this unit; press. Sew 2-1/2 x 7-1/2-inch **GOLD #2** rectangles to both side edges of the unit; press. Sew the Step 2 roof unit to the top edge of the house base; press.

Step 6 ✏ Sew the 1-1/2-inch **GOLD #2** squares to both side edges of the 1-1/2 x 6-1/2-inch **BROWN #1** rectangle; press. Sew the 1-1/2 x 8-1/2-inch **BLUE #2** rectangle to the bottom edge of this unit; press.

 Make 1

Step 7 ✏ With right sides together, position a 1-1/2-inch **BROWN #1** square on the corner of a 3-1/2-inch **BEIGE** square. Draw a diagonal line on the **BROWN #1** square; stitch, trim, and press. Make 2 units. Sew the units to both side edges of the 2-1/2 x 3-1/2-inch **BROWN #1** rectangle; press. *At this point the post unit should measure 3-1/2 x 8-1/2-inches.*

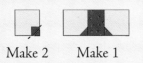

Make 2   Make 1

Step 8 ✏ Sew the Step 6 and Step 7 units to the bottom edge of the Step 5 house unit; press. *At this point the house unit should measure 8-1/2 x 16-1/2-inches.*

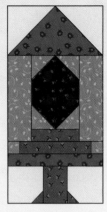

Make 1

Step 9 ✏ With right sides together, position a 2-1/2-inch **BEIGE** square on the corner of a 2-1/2 x 4-1/2-inch **BROWN #1** rectangle. Draw a diagonal line on the square; stitch, trim, and press. Repeat this process at the opposite corner of the rectangle. *At this point each flying geese unit should measure 2-1/2 x 4-1/2-inches.*

Make 3

Step 10 ✏ Repeat Step 9 using 2-1/2-inch **BEIGE** squares and a 2-1/2 x 4-1/2-inch **GOLD #2** rectangle.

 Make 3

Step 11 ✏ Repeat Step 9 using 2-1/2-inch **BEIGE** squares and a 2-1/2 x 4-1/2-inch **DARK BLUE** rectangle.

 Make 3

Step 12 ✎ Repeat Step 9 using 2-1/2-inch **BEIGE** squares and a 2-1/2 x 4-1/2-inch **BROWN #2** rectangle.

 Make 3

Step 13 ✎ Repeat Step 9 using 2-1/2-inch **BEIGE** squares and a 2-1/2 x 4-1/2-inch **RED #1** rectangle.

 Make 2

Step 14 ✎ Referring to the block diagram for color placement, sew 4 flying geese units together; press. Sew this unit to the top edge of the Step 8 house unit; press.

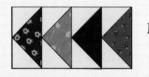 Make 1

Step 15 ✎ Referring to the block diagram, sew 10 flying geese units together; press. Sew this unit to the right edge of the Step 8 house unit; press.

Step 16 ✎ Referring to the block diagram, sew the Step 3 house to the top edge of the Step 4 house; press. Sew this unit to the left edge of the Step 15 unit; press. *At this point the block should measure 20-1/2-inches square.* Refer to **Appliqué the Birdhouse Holes** on page 150 for complete instructions on adding the birdhouse holes.

SAFE HAVEN Block 3

SAFE HAVEN
BLOCK - *Four*

CUTTING

From BEIGE PRINT:
❊ Cut 1, 2-7/8 x 42-inch strip.
   From the strip cut
      12, 2-7/8-inch squares
❊ Cut 1, 2-1/2 x 42-inch strip.
   From the strip cut:
      16, 2-1/2-inch squares

From BRICK PRINT #1:
❊ Cut 2, 2-1/2-inch squares

From CORAL PLAID:
❊ Cut 2, 2-1/2 x 35-inch strips.
   From the strips cut:
      2, 2-1/2-inch squares
      8, 2-1/2 x 4-1/2-inch rectangles

From EGGPLANT PRINT:
❊ Cut 1, 4-1/2 x 42-inch strip.
   From the strip cut:
      1, 4-1/2-inch square
      4, 2-1/2 x 4-1/2-inch rectangles
      4, 2-1/2-inch squares
      4, 1-1/2-inch squares

From LIGHT GREEN PRINT:
❊ Cut 4, 2-7/8-inch squares
❊ Cut 2, 2-1/2 x 42-inch strips.
   From the strips cut:
      4, 2-1/2 x 4-1/2-inch rectangles
      20, 2-1/2-inch squares
      8, 1-1/2-inch squares

From DARK GREEN PRINT:
❊ Cut 8, 2-7/8-inch squares
❊ Cut 1, 2-1/2 x 42-inch strip.
   From the strip cut:
      4, 2-1/2 x 4-1/2-inch rectangles
      4, 2-1/2-inch squares

From RED PRINT #2:
❊ Cut 1, 2-1/2 x 42-inch strip.
   From the strip cut:
      8, 2-1/2 x 4-1/2-inch rectangles

PIECING

Step 1 ✏ With right sides together, position a 1-1/2-inch **EGGPLANT** square on the corner of a 2-1/2-inch **BRICK #1** square. Draw a diagonal line on the **EGGPLANT** square; stitch, trim, and press. Make 2 units. Repeat this process using a 1-1/2-inch **EGGPLANT** square and a 2-1/2-inch **CORAL PLAID** square. Make 2 units.

Make 2   Make 2

Step 2 ✏ Sew the Step 1 units together in pairs; press. Sew the pairs together; press. *At this point the flower center should measure 4-1/2-inches square.*

Make 1

Step 3 ✏ With right sides together, position a 1-1/2-inch **LIGHT GREEN** square on the corner of a 2-1/2-inch **EGGPLANT** square. Draw a diagonal line on the **GREEN** square; stitch, trim, and press. Make 4 units. Sew the units together in pairs; press. Sew the pairs to the top/bottom edges of the Step 2 flower center; press.

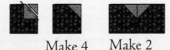

Make 4   Make 2

Step 4 ✏ With right sides together, position a 1-1/2-inch **LIGHT GREEN** square on the right corner of a 2-1/2 x 4-1/2-inch **EGGPLANT** rectangle. Draw a diagonal line on the square; stitch, trim, and press. Make 2 units. Position a 1-1/2-inch **LIGHT GREEN** square on the left corner of a 2-1/2 x 4-1/2-inch **EGGPLANT** rectangle. Draw a diagonal line on the square; stitch, trim, and press. Make 2 units. Sew the units together in pairs; press.

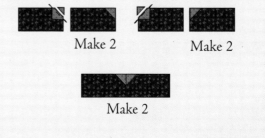

Make 2   Make 2

Make 2

(continued on the next page)

Step 5 ❧ Sew the Step 4 units to the side edges of the flower center; press. *At this point the flower should measure 8-1/2-inches square.*

 Make 1

Step 6 ❧ With right sides together, position a 2-1/2-inch **BEIGE** square on the corner of a 2-1/2 x 4-1/2-inch **LIGHT GREEN** rectangle. Draw a diagonal line on the square; stitch, trim, and press. Repeat this process at the opposite corner of the rectangle. *At this point each unit should measure 2-1/2 x 4-1/2-inches.*

 Make 4

Step 7 ❧ Repeat Step 6 using 2-1/2-inch **BEIGE** squares and 2-1/2 x 4-1/2-inch **DARK GREEN** rectangles.

 Make 4

Step 8 ❧ With right sides together, layer together the 2-7/8-inch **LIGHT GREEN** squares with 4 of the 2-7/8-inch **BEIGE** squares in pairs. Cut the layered squares in half

diagonally to make 8 sets of layered triangles. Stitch 1/4-inch from the diagonal edge of each pair of triangles; press. *At this point each triangle-pieced square should measure 2-1/2-inches square.*

 Make 8, 2-1/2-inch triangle-pieced squares

Step 9 ❧ Referring to the block diagram, sew the triangle-pieced squares to both side edges of the Step 6 units; press. Make 4 units. Sew a unit to the top/bottom edges of the Step 5 flower unit; press. Sew a 2-1/2-inch **LIGHT GREEN** square to both ends of the remaining units; press. Referring to the block diagram, sew the units to the side edges of the flower/leaf unit; press. *At this point the flower/leaf unit should measure 12-1/2-inches square.*

Make 4   Make 2

Step 10 ❧ Repeat Step 8 using the 2-7/8-inch **DARK GREEN** squares and 8 of the 2-7/8-inch **BEIGE** squares. Cut the layered squares in half diagonally to make 16 sets of layered triangles. Stitch and press each pair of triangles to make 16, 2-1/2-inch triangle-pieced squares. Sew the triangle-pieced squares together in pairs; press. Sew the pairs to both side edges of the Step 7 units; press. *At this point each unit should measure 2-1/2 x 12-1/2-inches.*

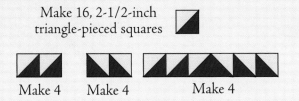

Make 16, 2-1/2-inch triangle-pieced squares

Make 4   Make 4   Make 4

Step 11 ✒ Sew a Step 10 unit to the top/bottom edges of the Step 9 flower/leaf unit; press. Sew a 2-1/2-inch **DARK GREEN** square to both ends of the remaining Step 10 units; press. Sew the units to the side edges of the flower/leaf unit; press. *At this point the flower/leaf unit should measure 16-1/2-inches square.*

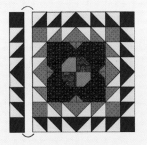

Step 12 ✒ Position a 2-1/2-inch **LIGHT GREEN** square on the corner of a 2-1/2 x 4-1/2-inch **RED #2** rectangle. Draw a diagonal line on the square; stitch, trim, and press. Repeat this process using a 2-1/2-inch **LIGHT GREEN**

square and a 2-1/2 x 4-1/2-inch **CORAL PLAID** rectangle. Notice the direction of the stitching line.

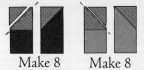

Make 8   Make 8

Step 13 ✒ Sew the Step 12 units together in pairs; press. Referring to the block diagram, sew 4 pairs together to make a fence section; press. Make 2 fence sections. *At this point each fence section should measure 4-1/2 x 16-1/2-inches.*

Make 8

Step 14 ✒ Referring to the block diagram, sew a fence section to the top edge of the Step 11 flower/leaf unit; press. Sew the 4-1/2-inch **EGGPLANT** square to the left edge of the remaining fence section; press. Sew the fence section to the right edge of the flower/leaf unit; press. *At this point the block should measure 20-1/2-inches square.*

Safe Haven Block 4

SAFE HAVEN
BLOCK - *Five*

CUTTING

From BEIGE PRINT:

❊ Cut 1, 6-7/8 x 42-inch strip.
　From the strip cut:
　　1, 6-7/8-inch square
　　2, 1-1/2 x 10-1/2-inch rectangles
　　4, 1-1/2-inch squares
❊ Cut 2, 2-7/8 x 30-inch strips

From DARK GREEN PRINT:

❊ Cut 2, 2-7/8 x 30-inch strips

From EGGPLANT PRINT:

❊ Cut 1, 2-7/8 x 42-inch strip.
　From the strip cut:
　　2, 2-7/8-inch squares
　　1, 2-5/8-inch square
　　1, 2-1/2 x 4-1/2-inch rectangle
　　3, 2-1/2-inch squares
❊ Cut 1, 1-1/2 x 42-inch strip.
　From the strip cut:
　　2, 1-1/2 x 8-1/2-inch rectangles
　　2, 1-1/2 x 10-1/2-inch rectangles

From LIGHT GREEN PRINT:

❊ Cut 1, 2-7/8 x 42-inch strip.
　From the strip cut:
　　2, 2-7/8-inch squares
　　1, 2-1/2 x 8-1/2-inch rectangle
　　1, 2-1/2 x 6-1/2-inch rectangle

　　1, 2-1/2 x 4-1/2-inch rectangle
　　1, 2-1/2-inch square
　　1, 1 x 4-1/2-inch rectangle

From BLUE PRINT #2:

❊ Cut 1, 6-7/8-inch square
❊ Cut 1, 2-1/2 x 12-1/2-inch rectangle

From BRICK PRINT #1:

❊ Cut 2, 4-1/2-inch squares

PIECING

Step 1 ✎ With right sides together, layer together the 2-7/8 x 30-inch **DARK GREEN** and **BEIGE** strips in pairs. Press together, but do not sew. Cut the layered strips into 18, 2-7/8-inch squares. Cut each layered square in half diagonally to make 36 sets of layered triangles. Stitch 1/4-inch from the diagonal edge of each pair of triangles; press. *At this point each triangle-pieced square should measure 2-1/2-inches square.*

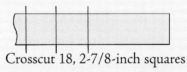

Crosscut 18, 2-7/8-inch squares

Make 36, 2-1/2-inch triangle-pieced squares

Step 2 ✒ Sew 3 triangle-pieced squares together; press. Make 10 units. Referring to the block diagram, sew the units together to make the side sawtooth unit; press. *At this point the sawtooth unit should measure 6-1/2 x 20-1/2-inches.* Sew the remaining 6 triangle-pieced squares together for the bottom sawtooth unit; press.

Make 10

Make 1 bottom sawtooth unit

Step 3 ✒ With right sides together, position the 2-1/2 x 4-1/2-inch **EGGPLANT** rectangle on the left corner of the 2-1/2 x 4-1/2-inch **LIGHT GREEN** rectangle. Draw a diagonal line on the **EGGPLANT** rectangle; stitch, trim, and press. *At this point the unit should measure 2-1/2 x 6-1/2-inches.*

Make 1

Step 4 ✒ To make the stem unit, cut the 2-5/8-inch **EGGPLANT** square in half diagonally. Center an **EGGPLANT** triangle on the 1 x 4-1/2-inch **LIGHT GREEN** rectangle; stitch a 1/4-inch seam. Center the remaining **EGGPLANT** triangle on the opposite edge of the **LIGHT GREEN** rectangle; stitch. Press the seam allowances toward the **LIGHT GREEN** rectangle. Trim the stem unit so it measures

2-1/2-inches square. Sew the stem unit to the right edge of the Step 3 unit; press. *At this point the unit should measure 2-1/2 x 8-1/2-inches.*

Trim   Make 1

Make 1

Step 5 ✒ With right sides together, position a 2-1/2-inch **EGGPLANT** square on the left corner of the 2-1/2 x 8-1/2-inch **LIGHT GREEN** rectangle. Draw a diagonal line on the square; stitch, trim, and press. *At this point the unit should measure 2-1/2 x 8-1/2-inches.*

Make 1

(continued on the next page)

BLOCK *Five* Continued

Step 6 ✒ With right sides together, position a 2-1/2-inch **EGGPLANT** square on the left corner of the 2-1/2 x 6-1/2-inch **LIGHT GREEN** rectangle. Draw a diagonal line on the square; stitch, trim, and press.

Make 1

Step 7 ✒ With right sides together, layer 2 of the 2-7/8-inch **EGGPLANT** squares and 2 of the 2-7/8-inch **LIGHT GREEN** squares in pairs. Cut each layered square in half diagonally to make 4 sets of layered triangles. Stitch 1/4-inch from the diagonal edge of each pair of triangles; press. *At this point each triangle-pieced square should measure 2-1/2-inches square. You will be using only 3 triangle-pieced squares.* Sew 1 triangle-pieced square to the right edge of the Step 6 unit; press. *At this point the unit should measure 2-1/2 x 8-1/2-inches.*

Make 3, 2-1/2-inch triangle-pieced squares

Make 1

Step 8 ✒ Sew 2 triangle-pieced squares together. Sew the 2-1/2-inch **LIGHT GREEN** square to the left edge of the unit. Sew a 2-1/2-inch **EGGPLANT** square to the right edge of the unit; press. *At this point the unit should measure 2-1/2 x 8-1/2-inches.*

Make 1

Step 9 ✒ Sew the Step 4, 5, 7, and 8 units together; press. *At this point the leaf block should measure 8-1/2-inches square.* Sew the 1-1/2 x 8-1/2-inch **EGGPLANT** rectangles to the top/bottom edges of the leaf block; press. Sew the 1-1/2 x 10-1/2-inch **EGGPLANT** and **BEIGE** rectangles to the side edges of the block; press. *At this point the house unit should measure 10-1/2 x 12-1/2-inches.*

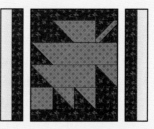

Make 1

Step 10 ✒ With right sides together, layer the 6-7/8-inch **BEIGE** and **BLUE #2** squares. Cut the layered square in half diagonally to make 2 sets of layered triangles. Stitch 1/4-inch from the diagonal edge of each pair of triangles; press. Position a 4-1/2-inch **BRICK #1** square on the **BLUE** side of each triangle-pieced square. Draw a diagonal line on the **BRICK #1** square; stitch, trim, and press. Sew the triangle-pieced squares together to make the roof unit; press. *At this point the roof unit should measure 6-1/2 x 12-1/2-inches.*

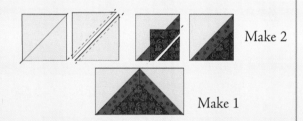

Make 2

Make 1

Step 11 ✔ With right sides together, position 1-1/2-inch **BEIGE** squares on opposite corners of the 2-1/2 x 12-1/2-inch **BLUE #2** rectangle. Draw a diagonal line on the **BEIGE** squares; stitch, trim, and press. Repeat this process for the remaining corner of the rectangle. Sew the 6-piece sawtooth unit to the bottom edge of this unit; press. *At this point the base unit should measure 4-1/2 x 12-1/2-inches.* (see diagram in next column)

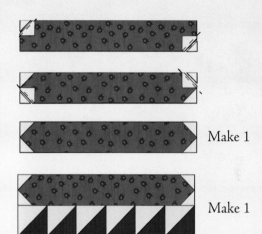

Make 1

Make 1

Step 12 ✔ Sew the roof unit to the top edge of the house unit; press. Sew the base unit to the bottom edge; press. Sew the Step 2 side sawtooth unit to the house block; press. *At this point the block should measure 18-1/2 x 20-1/2-inches.* Refer to **Appliqué the Birdhouse Holes** on page 150 for complete instructions on adding the birdhouse hole.

SAFE HAVEN Block 5

SAFE HAVEN
BLOCK - *Six*

CUTTING

From BEIGE PRINT:
❊ Cut 3, 2-1/2 x 42-inch strips.
  From the strips cut:
    16, 2-1/2 x 4-1/2-inch rectangles
    16, 2-1/2-inch squares
❊ Cut 1 more 2-1/2 x 42-inch strip

From ROSE PRINT:
❊ Cut 1, 2-1/2 x 42-inch strip
❊ Cut 4, 2-1/2-inch squares

From DARK GREEN PRINT:
❊ Cut 1, 2-1/2 x 42-inch strip.
  From the strip cut:
    16, 2-1/2-inch squares
❊ Cut 1, 1 x 42-inch strip.
  From the strip cut:
    24, 1-inch squares

From LIGHT GOLD PRINT:
❊ Cut 2, 1-1/2 x 14-inch strips.
  From the strips cut:
    16, 1-1/2-inch squares

From PLUM PRINT #1:
❊ Cut 4, 2-1/2-inch squares

From PLUM PRINT #2:
❊ Cut 4, 2-1/2-inch squares

From RED PRINT #2:
❊ Cut 4, 2-1/2-inch squares

From LIGHT GREEN PRINT:
❊ Cut 1, 2-1/2 x 42-inch strip.
  From the strip cut:
    16, 2-1/2-inch squares
❊ Cut 1, 1 x 42-inch strip.
  From the strip cut:
    24, 1-inch squares

Piecing

Step 1 ✒ Aligning long edges, sew the 2-1/2 x 42-inch **ROSE** and **BEIGE** strips together; press. Cut the strip set into segments.

Crosscut 13, 2-1/2-inch wide segments

Step 2 ✒ Sew 4 of the Step 1 segments together side by side to make the top and bottom checkerboard units; press. Sew the remaining 5, Step 1 segments together end to end to make the center checkerboard unit; press.

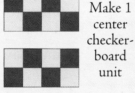

Make 1 top checkerboard unit

Make 1 bottom checkerboard unit

Make 1 center checker-board unit

Step 3 ✒ With right sides together, position 1-inch **DARK GREEN** squares on 3 corners of a 2-1/2-inch **ROSE** square. Draw a diagonal line on the **DARK GREEN** squares; stitch, trim, and press. Position a 1-1/2-inch **LIGHT GOLD** square on the remaining corner of the **ROSE** square. Draw a diagonal line on the **LIGHT GOLD** square; stitch, trim, and press.

Sew the 4 units together to make the flower center; press. *At this point the flower center should measure 4-1/2-inches square.*

Make 4

Make 1

Step 4 ✒ With right sides together, position a 2-1/2-inch **DARK GREEN** square on the corner of a 2-1/2 x 4-1/2-inch **BEIGE** rectangle. Draw a diagonal line on the square; stitch, trim, and press. Repeat this process at the opposite corner of the rectangle. *At this point each unit should measure 2-1/2 x 4-1/2-inches.*

Make 4

(continued on the next page).

Step 5 ✎ Sew Step 4 units to the top/bottom edges of the Step 3 flower center; press. Sew 2-1/2-inch **BEIGE** squares to both ends of the remaining Step 4 units; press. Sew the units to the side edges of the flower center; press. *At this point the flower unit should measure 8-1/2-inches square.*

 Make 1

Step 6 ✎ Referring to the Step 3, 4, and 5 diagrams and instructions, make the remaining 3 flower units. Use 2-1/2-inch **PLUM #1, PLUM #2,** and **RED #2** squares for the flower centers and 1-inch and 2-1/2-inch **DARK** and **LIGHT GREEN** squares for the flower petals. The 1-1/2-inch **LIGHT GOLD** squares, 2-1/2-inch **BEIGE** squares, and 2-1/2 x 4-1/2-inch **BEIGE** rectangles remain the same.

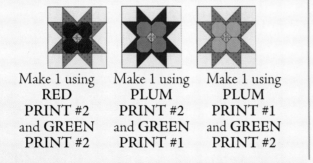

| Make 1 using **RED PRINT #2** and **GREEN PRINT #2** | Make 1 using **PLUM PRINT #2** and **GREEN PRINT #1** | Make 1 using **PLUM PRINT #1** and **GREEN PRINT #2** |

Step 7 ✎ Sew the flower blocks together in pairs; press. Sew a top and bottom checkerboard unit to each of the flower block units; press. *At this point each unit should measure 8-1/2 x 20-1/2-inches.*

Step 8 ✎ Referring to the block diagram, sew the Step 7 flower/checkerboard units to both side edges of the center checkerboard unit; press. *At this point the block should measure 18-1/2 x 20-1/2-inches.*

SAFE HAVEN Block 6

Safe Haven
Block - *Seven*

CUTTING

From BEIGE PRINT:
❊ Cut 1, 3-1/2 x 42-inch strip.
   From the strip cut:
      6, 3-1/2-inch squares
      3, 2-7/8-inch squares
      3, 2-5/8-inch squares
❊ Cut 6, 2-1/2-inch squares

From BROWN PRINT #1:
❊ Cut 1, 4-1/2 x 22-inch strip.
   From the strip cut:
      1, 4-1/2 x 6-1/2-inch rectangle
      1, 3-1/2 x 6-1/2-inch rectangle
      2, 1-1/2 x 6-1/2-inch rectangles

From RED PLAID:
❊ Cut 1, 3-1/2 x 6-1/2-inch rectangle
❊ Cut 1, 1-1/2 x 6-1/2-inch rectangle

From BLUE PRINT #1:
❊ Cut 1, 3-1/2 x 6-1/2-inch rectangle
❊ Cut 2, 1-1/2 x 6-1/2-inch rectangles

From GOLD PRINT #1 and GOLD PRINT #2:
❊ Cut 1, 4-1/2 x 6-1/2-inch rectangle each

From BROWN PLAID:
❊ Cut 1, 5-1/2 x 6-1/2-inch rectangle

From EGGPLANT PRINT and RED PRINT #1:
❊ Cut 1, 5-1/2 x 6-1/2-inch rectangle each

From DARK GREEN PRINT:
❊ Cut 1, 2-7/8 x 30-inch strip.
   From the strip cut:
      1, 2-7/8-inch square
      1, 2-1/2 x 6-1/2-inch rectangle
      1, 2-1/2 x 4-1/2-inch rectangle
      1, 2-1/2-inch square
      1, 1-1/2 x 6-1/2-inch rectangle
      1, 1 x 4-1/2-inch rectangle

From LIGHT GREEN PRINT:
❊ Cut 1, 2-7/8 x 42-inch strip.
   From the strip cut:
      1, 2-7/8-inch square
      1, 2-1/2 x 6-1/2-inch rectangle
      1, 2-1/2 x 4-1/2-inch rectangle
      1, 2-1/2-inch square
      1, 1 x 4-1/2-inch rectangle

From RED PRINT #2:
❊ Cut 1, 2-7/8 x 42-inch strip.
   From the strip cut:
      1, 2-7/8-inch square
      1, 2-1/2 x 6-1/2-inch rectangle
      1, 2-1/2 x 4-1/2-inch rectangle
      1, 2-1/2-inch square
      1, 1 x 4-1/2-inch rectangle

PIECING

Step 1 ✎ With right sides together, position a 3-1/2-inch **BEIGE** square on the corner of the 3-1/2 x 6-1/2-inch **BROWN #1** rectangle. Draw a diagonal line on the square; stitch, trim, and press. Repeat this process at the opposite corner of the rectangle. *At this point the roof unit should measure 3-1/2 x 6-1/2-inches.*

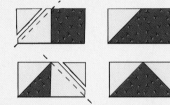

Make 1

Step 2 ✎ Repeat Step 1 to make the **RED PLAID** roof and the **DARK BLUE** roof.

Step 3 ✎ Sew together the 4-1/2 x 6-1/2-inch **GOLD #1** rectangle, the 1-1/2 x 6-1/2-inch **BLUE #1** rectangle, the 5-1/2 x 6-1/2-inch **BROWN PLAID** rectangle, and the 1-1/2 x 6-1/2-inch **BROWN #1** rectangle. Press the seam allowances all one way. Sew the **BROWN #1** roof unit to the top edge of this unit; press. *At this point the house unit should measure 6-1/2 x 14-1/2-inches.*

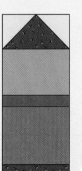

Make 1

Step 4 ✎ Sew together the 5-1/2 x 6-1/2-inch **EGGPLANT** rectangle, the 1-1/2 x 6-1/2-inch **BROWN #1** rectangle, the 4-1/2 x 6-1/2-inch **GOLD #2** rectangle, and the 1-1/2 x 6-1/2-inch **RED PLAID** rectangle. Press the seam allowances opposite from the Step 3 house. Sew the **RED PLAID** roof unit to the top of this unit; press. *At this point the house unit should measure 6-1/2 x 14-1/2-inches.*

Make 1

(continued on the next page)

Step 5 ✒ Sew together the 4-1/2 x 6-1/2-inch **BROWN #1** rectangle, the 1-1/2 x 6-1/2-inch **DARK GREEN** rectangle, the 5-1/2 x 6-1/2-inch **RED #1** rectangle, and the 1-1/2 x 6-1/2-inch **DARK BLUE** rectangle. Press the seam allowance opposite from Step 4 house. Sew the **BLUE #1** roof unit to the top edge of this unit; press. *At this point the house unit should measure 6-1/2 x 14-1/2-inches.*

Make 1

Step 6 ✒ Referring to the block diagram, sew the Step 3, 4, and 5 house units together; press.

Step 7 ✒ With right sides together, position a 2-1/2-inch **BEIGE** square on the right corner of the 2-1/2 x 4-1/2-inch **DARK GREEN** rectangle. Draw a diagonal line on the square; stitch, trim, and press.

Make 1

Step 8 ✒ To make the stem unit, cut the 2-5/8-inch **BEIGE** square in half diagonally. Center a **BEIGE** triangle on the 1 x 4-1/2-inch **DARK GREEN**

rectangle; stitch a 1/4-inch seam. Center the remaining **BEIGE** triangle on the opposite edge of the **GREEN** rectangle; stitch. Press the seam allowance toward the **GREEN** rectangle. Trim the stem unit so it measures 2-1/2-inches square. Sew the stem unit to the left edge of the Step 7 unit; press. *At this point the unit should measure 2-1/2 x 6-1/2-inches.*

Trim   Make 1   Make 1

Step 9 ✒ With right sides together, position a 2-1/2-inch **BEIGE** square on the right corner of the 2-1/2 x 6-1/2-inch **DARK GREEN** rectangle. Draw a diagonal line on the square; stitch, trim, and press. *At this point the unit should measure 2-1/2 x 6-1/2-inches.*

Make 1

Step 10 ✒ With right sides together, layer the 2-7/8-inch **DARK GREEN** and **BEIGE** squares. Cut the layered square in half diagonally to make 2 sets of layered triangles. Stitch 1/4-inch from the diagonal edge of each pair of triangles; press. *At this point each triangle-pieced square should measure 2-1/2-inches square.*

 Make 2, 2-1/2-inch triangle-pieced squares

Step 11 ✒ Sew the Step 10 triangle-pieced squares together. Sew the 2-1/2-inch **DARK GREEN** square to the right edge; press. *At this point the unit should measure 2-1/2 x 6-1/2-inches.*

 Make 1

Step 12 ✒ Sew the Step 8, 9, and 11 units together to complete the leaf unit; press. *At this point the leaf unit should measure 6-1/2-inches square.*

 Make 1

Step 13 ✒ Repeat Steps 7 through 12 using the **RED #2** and **BEIGE** fabrics to make one leaf and the **LIGHT GREEN** and **BEIGE** fabrics to make another leaf.

Step 14 ✒ Referring to the block diagram, sew the leaf units together; press. Sew the Step 6 house unit to the top edge of the leaf unit; press. *At this point the block should measure 18-1/2 x 20-1/2-inches.* Refer to **Appliqué the Birdhouse Holes** on page 150 for complete instructions on adding the birdhouse holes.

SAFE HAVEN Block 7

SAFE HAVEN
BLOCK - *Eight*

CUTTING

From BEIGE PRINT:
❋ Cut 1, 6-1/2 x 42-inch strip.
   From the strip cut:
      2, 6-1/2-inch squares.
   From the remainder of the strip cut:
      4, 1-1/2 x 29-inch strips.
   From the strips cut:
      24, 1-1/2 x 2-1/2-inch rectangles
      28, 1-1/2-inch squares
❋ Cut 1, 1-1/2 x 42-inch strip.
   From the strip cut:
      20, 1-1/2-inch squares

From LIGHT GOLD PRINT:
❋ Cut 4, 2-1/2 x 4-1/2-inch rectangles

From RED PLAID:
❋ Cut 1, 4-1/2-inch square
❋ Cut 8, 2-1/2-inch squares

From BROWN PRINT #1:
❋ Cut 2, 2-1/2 x 21-inch strips.
   From the strips cut:
      16, 2-1/2-inch squares

From BLUE PRINT #1:
❋ Cut 2, 2-1/2 x 42-inch strips.
   From the strips cut:
      8, 2-1/2 x 4-1/2-inch rectangles
      5, 2-1/2-inch squares

From BLUE PRINT #2:
❋ Cut 1, 6-1/2 x 12-1/2-inch rectangle

From GOLD PRINT #1:
❋ Cut 2, 1-1/2 x 32-inch strips.
   From the strips cut:
      7, 1-1/2 x 3-1/2-inch rectangles
      14, 1-1/2-inch squares

From GOLD PRINT #2:
❋ Cut 2, 1-1/2 x 30-inch strips.
   From the strips cut:
      5, 1-1/2 x 3-1/2-inch rectangles
      10, 1-1/2-inch squares

From MEDIUM GREEN PRINT:
❋ Cut 4, 2-1/2-inch squares

PIECING

Step 1 ❧ Sew a 2-1/2 x 4-1/2-inch **LIGHT GOLD** rectangle to the top/bottom edges of the 4-1/2-inch **RED PLAID** square; press. Sew 2-1/2-inch **RED PLAID** squares to the remaining 2-1/2 x 4-1/2-inch **LIGHT GOLD** rectangles; press. Sew the units to the side edges of the **RED PLAID** square; press. *At this point the unit should measure 8-1/2-inches square.*

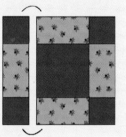

Make 1

Step 2 ❧ With right sides together, position a 2-1/2-inch **BROWN #1** square on the corner of a 2-1/2 x 4-1/2-inch **BLUE #1** rectangle. Draw a diagonal line on the square; stitch, trim, and press. Repeat this process at the opposite corner of the rectangle. Sew the units together in pairs; press. *At this point each unit should measure 2-1/2 x 8-1/2-inches.*

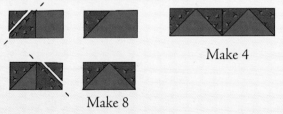

Make 4

Make 8

Step 3 ❧ Sew Step 2 units to the top/bottom edges of the Step 1 unit; press. Sew 2-1/2-inch **RED PLAID** squares to the remaining Step 2 units; press. Sew the units to the side edges of the Step 1 unit; press. *At this point the house section should measure 12-1/2-inches square.*

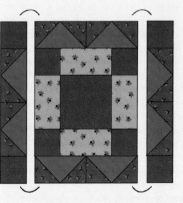

Make 1

(continued on the next page)

BLOCK - *Eight* Continued

Step 4 ✒ With right sides together, position a 6-1/2-inch **BEIGE** square on the corner of the 6-1/2 x 12-1/2-inch **BLUE #2** rectangle. Draw a diagonal line on the square; stitch, trim, and press. Repeat this process at the opposite corner of the rectangle. Sew the roof unit to the top edge of the Step 3 house unit; press. *At this point the house unit should measure 12-1/2 x 18-1/2-inches.*

Make 1

Step 5 ✒ With right sides together, position a 1-1/2-inch **GOLD #1** square on the right corner of a 1-1/2 x 2-1/2-inch **BEIGE** rectangle. Draw a diagonal line on the square; stitch, trim, and press. Sew a 1-1/2-inch **BEIGE** square to the right edge of this unit; press.

Make 14 using
GOLD PRINT #1

Step 6 ✒ With right sides together, position 1-1/2-inch **BEIGE** squares on the corners of a 1-1/2 x 3-1/2-inch **GOLD #1** rectangle. Draw a diagonal

line on the squares; stitch, trim, and press.

Make 7 using
GOLD PRINT #1

Step 7 ✒ Sew the Step 5 units to the top/bottom edges of the Step 6 units; press. *At this point each star unit should measure 3-1/2-inches square.*

Make 7 using
GOLD PRINT #1

Step 8 ✒ Repeat Steps 5, 6, and 7 to make the remaining star units, using the **GOLD #2** squares and rectangles and the remaining **BEIGE** squares and rectangles.

Make 7 using
GOLD PRINT #2

Step 9 ✒ Referring to the block diagram, sew the Step 7 and 8 star units together in 2 vertical strips; press. *At this point each star strip should measure 3-1/2 x 18-1/2-inches.*

Step 10 ✐ To make the checkerboard unit, sew together the 2-1/2-inch **BLUE #1** and **MEDIUM GREEN** squares; press. *At this point the checkerboard unit should measure 2-1/2 x 18-1/2-inches.*

Make 1

Step 11 ✐ Referring to the block diagram, sew the Step 9 star strips to both side edges of the Step 4 house unit; press. Sew the Step 10 checkerboard unit to the bottom edge of the unit; press. *At this point the block should measure 18-1/2 x 20-1/2-inches.* Refer to **Appliqué the Birdhouse Holes** on page 150 for complete instructions on adding the birdhouse hole.

SAFE HAVEN Block 8

Safe Haven
Block - *Nine*

Cutting

From BEIGE PRINT:
❋ Cut 1, 5-1/4 x 42-inch strip.
   From the strip cut:
      2, 5-1/4-inch squares.
         Cut the squares diagonally into
         quarters, to make 8 triangles. You
         will be using only 6 of the triangles.
      2, 4-1/2-inch squares
❋ Cut 1, 2-7/8 x 42-inch strip

From GOLD PRINT #2:
❋ Cut 1, 5-1/4 x 42-inch strip.
   From the strip cut:
      2, 5-1/4-inch squares.
         Cut the squares diagonally into
         quarters, to make 8 triangles. You
         will be using only 6 of the triangles.
      1, 4-1/2 x 8-1/2-inch rectangle
      2, 4-1/2-inch squares
      4, 1-1/2-inch squares

From BROWN PRINT #1:
❋ Cut 1, 4-1/2 x 10-1/2-inch rectangle

From ROSE PRINT:
❋ Cut 1, 7-1/2 x 8-1/2-inch rectangle
❋ Cut 2, 1-1/2 x 4-1/2-inch rectangles

From MEDIUM GREEN PRINT:
❋ Cut 1, 2-1/2 x 6-1/2-inch rectangle

From BLUE PRINT #1:
❋ Cut 1, 2-1/2 x 6-1/2-inch rectangle

From RED PRINT #2:
❋ Cut 1, 2-1/2 x 6-1/2-inch rectangle

From DARK GREEN PRINT:
❋ Cut 1, 2-1/2 x 6-1/2-inch rectangle

From DARK BLUE PRINT:
❋ Cut 1, 2-7/8 x 42-inch strip
❋ Cut 2, 2-1/2 x 42-inch strips.
   From the strips cut:
      2, 2-1/2 x 18-1/2-inch strips
      1, 2-1/2 x 20-1/2-inch strip

PIECING

Step 1 ❧ With right sides together, position a 4-1/2-inch **BEIGE** square on the left corner of the 4-1/2 x 8-1/2-inch **GOLD #2** rectangle. Draw a diagonal line on the square; stitch, trim, and press. Referring to the diagram, position the 4-1/2 x 10-1/2-inch **BROWN #1** rectangle on the right corner of the **GOLD #2** rectangle. Draw a diagonal line on the upper corner of the **BROWN #1** rectangle; stitch, trim, and press.

Make 1

Step 2 ❧ With right sides together, position a 4-1/2-inch **BEIGE** square on the right corner of the Step 1 unit. Draw a diagonal line on the square; stitch, trim, and press. *At this point the roof unit should measure 4-1/2 x 14-1/2-inches.*

Make 1

Step 3 ❧ Sew together the 2-1/2 x 6-1/2-inch **MEDIUM GREEN, BLUE #1, RED #2,** and **DARK GREEN** rectangles; press. *At this point the unit should measure 6-1/2 x 8-1/2-inches.*

Make 1

Step 4 ❧ With right sides together, position a 4-1/2-inch **GOLD #2** square on the left corner of the 7-1/2 x 8-1/2-inch **ROSE** rectangle. Draw a diagonal line on the square; stitch, trim, and press. Repeat this process at the adjacent corner of the **ROSE** rectangle.

7-1/2"

Make 1

(continued on the next page)

Step 5 ✒ With right sides together, position 1-1/2-inch **GOLD #2** squares on the corners of the 1-1/2 x 4-1/2-inch **ROSE** rectangle. Draw a diagonal line on the squares; stitch, trim, and press. Make 2 units. Sew the 2 units together; press. Sew this unit to the top edge of the Step 4 unit; press. *At this point the heart unit should measure 8-1/2-inches square.*

Make 2

Make 1

Step 6 ✒ Sew the Step 5 heart unit to the left edge of the Step 3 unit; press. Sew the Step 2 roof unit to the top edge of this unit; press. *At this point the house unit should measure 12-1/2 x 14-1/2-inches.*

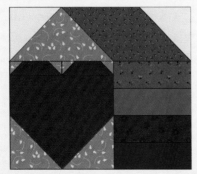

Make 1

Step 7 ✒ Layer a **GOLD #2** triangle on a **BEIGE** triangle. Stitch along the bias edge; press. Repeat with the remaining **GOLD #2** and **BEIGE** triangles, stitching along the same bias edge of each triangle set. Make 6 triangle units. Sew the triangle units together in pairs; press. *At this point each pieced triangle square should measure 4-1/2-inches square.*

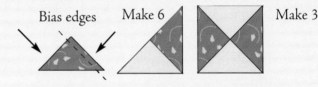

Bias edges · Make 6 · Make 3

Step 8 ✒ Referring to the block diagram, sew the Step 7 triangle squares together; press. Sew this unit to the right edge of the Step 6 house unit; press. *At this point the unit should measure 12-1/2 x 18-1/2-inches.*

Step 9 ✒ With right sides together, layer together the 2-7/8 x 42-inch **DARK BLUE** and **BEIGE** strips. Press together, but do not sew. Cut the layered strips into squares. Cut each layered square in half diagonally to make 18 sets of layered triangles. Stitch 1/4-inch from the diagonal edge of each pair of triangles; press. *At this point each triangle-pieced square should measure 2-1/2-inches square.*

Crosscut 9, 2-7/8-inch squares

Make 18, 2-1/2-inch
triangle-pieced squares

Step 10 ✒ Sew 9 of the Step 9 triangle-pieced squares together; press. Make another strip. Sew the sawtooth strips to the top/bottom edges of the Step 8 unit; press.

Step 11 ✒ Referring to the block diagram, sew a 2-1/2 x 18-1/2-inch **DARK BLUE** strip to the top/bottom edges of the Step 10 unit; press. Sew the 2-1/2 x 20-1/2-inch **DARK BLUE** strip to the left edge of the unit to complete the block; press. *At this point the block should measure 20-1/2-inches square.* Refer to **Appliqué the Birdhouse Holes** on page 150 for complete instructions on adding the birdhouse hole.

SAFE HAVEN Block 9

SAFE HAVEN
BLOCK - *Ten*

CUTTING

From BEIGE PRINT:
❋ Cut 1, 8-7/8-inch square
❋ Cut 2, 2-1/2 x 10-1/2-inch rectangles

From BLUE PRINT #2:
❋ Cut 1, 8-7/8-inch square
❋ Cut 1, 4-7/8-inch square
❋ Cut 1, 2-1/2 x 16-1/2-inch rectangle

From BROWN PLAID:
❋ Cut 2, 6-1/2-inch squares

From BROWN PRINT #2:
❋ Cut 1, 4-7/8-inch square
❋ Cut 2, 2-1/2 x 10-1/2-inch rectangles
❋ Cut 1, 2-1/2 x 27-inch strip

From RED PRINT #1:
❋ Cut 2, 3-1/2-inch squares
❋ Cut 1, 2-1/2 x 42-inch strip.
   From the strip cut:
      2, 2-1/2 x 6-1/2-inch rectangles
      1, 2-1/2 x 27-inch strip
❋ Cut 2, 1-1/2-inch squares

From LIGHT GOLD PRINT:
❋ Cut 1, 4-1/2 x 6-1/2-inch rectangle

PIECING

Step 1 ↝ With right sides together, layer the 8-7/8-inch **BEIGE** and **BLUE #2** squares. Cut the layered square in half diagonally to make 2 sets of layered triangles. Stitch 1/4-inch from the diagonal edge of each pair of triangles; press.

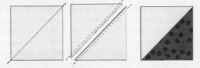

Make 2, 8-1/2-inch triangle-pieced squares

Step 2 ↝ With right sides together, position a 6-1/2-inch **BROWN PLAID** square on the **BLUE #2** side of each Step 1 triangle-pieced square. Draw a diagonal line on the **BROWN PLAID** square; stitch, trim, and press. Sew the triangle-pieced squares together to make the roof unit; press. *At this point the roof unit should measure 8-1/2 x 16-1/2-inches.*

Make 2

Step 3 ↝ With right sides together, layer the 4-7/8-inch **BROWN #2** and **BLUE #2** squares. Cut the layered

square in half diagonally to make 2 sets of layered triangles. Stitch 1/4-inch from the diagonal edge of each pair of triangles; press. Position a 3-1/2-inch **RED #1** square on the **BLUE #2** side of each triangle-pieced square. Draw a diagonal line on the **RED #1** square; stitch, trim, and press. Sew the triangle-pieced squares together to make the roof unit; press. *At this point the roof unit should measure 4-1/2 x 8-1/2-inches.*

Make 2, 4-1/2-inch triangle-pieced squares

Make 2

Make 1

Step 4 ✌ With right sides together, position 1-1/2-inch **RED #1** squares on the upper corners of the 4-1/2 x 6-1/2-inch **LIGHT GOLD** rectangle. Draw a diagonal line on the **RED #1** squares; stitch, trim, and press. Sew the 2-1/2 x 6-1/2-inch **RED #1** rectangles to both side edges of this unit; press. Sew the Step 3 roof unit to the top edge

of this unit; press. *At this point the unit should measure 8-1/2 x 10-1/2-inches.*

 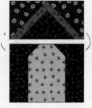

Make 1   Make 1

Step 5 ✌ Sew the 2-1/2 x 10-1/2-inch **BEIGE** and **BROWN #2** rectangles together in pairs; press. Sew the pairs to both side edges of the Step 4 unit; press. Sew the Step 2 roof unit to the top edge of this unit; press. *At this point the house unit should measure 16-1/2 x 18-1/2-inches.*

Make 1

141

(continued on the next page)

Step 6 ✒ Aligning long edges, sew the 2-1/2 x 27-inch **RED #1** and **BROWN #2** strips together; press. Cut the strip set into segments.

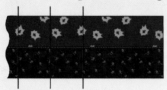

Crosscut 10, 2-1/2-inch wide segments

Step 7 ✒ Sew 5 of the Step 6 segments together end to end; press. Make 2 strips. *At this point each checkerboard strip should measure 2-1/2 x 20-1/2-inches.*

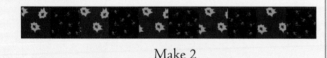

Make 2

Step 8 ✒ Referring to the block diagram, sew the 2-1/2 x 16-1/2-inch **BLUE #2** rectangle to the bottom edge of the Step 5 house unit; press. Sew the Step 7 checkerboard strips to both side edges of this unit to complete the block; press. *At this point the block should measure 20-1/2-inches square.* Refer to **Appliqué the Birdhouse Holes** on page 150 for complete instructions on adding the birdhouse holes.

SAFE HAVEN Block 10

SAFE HAVEN
BLOCK - *Eleven*

CUTTING

From BEIGE PRINT:
❋ Cut 1, 5-1/4 x 42-inch strip.
From the strip cut:
2, 5-1/4-inch squares. Cut the squares
diagonally into quarters to make 8
triangles.
1, 4-7/8-inch square
2, 2-7/8 x 14-inch strips
❋ Cut 1, 2-1/2 x 42-inch strip.
From the strip cut:
2, 2-1/2 x 10-1/2-inch rectangles
2, 2-1/2 x 6-1/2-inch rectangles

From BRICK PRINT #2:
❋ Cut 1, 4-7/8-inch square
❋ Cut 1, 2-1/2 x 8-1/2-inch rectangle
❋ Cut 10, 2-1/2-inch squares

From GOLD PRINT #2:
❋ Cut 1, 2-1/2 x 4-1/2-inch rectangle
❋ Cut 1, 2-1/2 x 8-1/2-inch rectangle

From RED PRINT #2:
❋ Cut 2, 5-1/4-inch squares. Cut the
squares diagonally into quarters to make
8 triangles.

From EGGPLANT PRINT:
❋ Cut 2, 2-1/2 x 10-1/2-inch rectangles
❋ Cut 1, 2-1/2 x 8-1/2-inch rectangle

From PLUM PRINT #2:
❋ Cut 8, 2-1/2-inch squares

From DARK GREEN PRINT:
❋ Cut 1, 4-1/2-inch square
❋ Cut 1, 2-7/8 x 14-inch strip

From MEDIUM GREEN PRINT:
❋ Cut 1, 2-7/8 x 14-inch strip

PIECING

Step 1 ✍ With right sides together, layer
the 4-7/8-inch **BEIGE** and **BRICK #2**
squares. Cut the layered square in half
diagonally to make 2 sets of layered
triangles. Stitch 1/4-inch from the
diagonal edge of each pair of triangles to
make 2 triangle-pieced squares; press.
*At this point each triangle-pieced square should
measure 4-1/2-inches square.*

Make 2, 4-1/2-inch triangle-pieced squares

Step 2 ✍ Sew 2-1/2-inch **BRICK #2**
squares to both side edges of the
2-1/2 x 4-1/2-inch **GOLD #2** rectangle;
press. Sew the 2-1/2 x 8-1/2-inch
GOLD #2 rectangle to the bottom edge
of this unit; press. Sew the Step 1

triangle-pieced squares to both side edges of this unit; press. *At this point the unit should measure 4-1/2 x 16-1/2-inches.*

Make 1

Step 3 ✎ With right sides together, position 2-1/2 x 6-1/2-inch **BEIGE** rectangles on the corners of the 2-1/2 x 8-1/2-inch **BRICK #2** rectangle. Draw a diagonal line on the upper edge of the **BEIGE** rectangles; stitch, trim, and press. Sew this unit to the top edge of the Step 2 unit; press. *At this point the roof unit should measure 6-1/2 x 16-1/2-inches.*

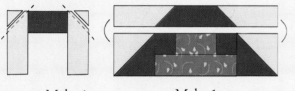

Make 1   Make 1

Step 4 ✎ Layer a **RED #2** triangle on a **BEIGE** triangle. Stitch along the bias edge; press. Repeat with the remaining **RED #2** and **BEIGE** triangles, stitching along the same bias edge of each triangle set. Make 8 triangle units. Sew the triangle units together in pairs; press. *At this point each pieced triangle square should measure 4-1/2-inches square.*

Bias edges

Make 8   Make 4

Step 5 ✎ Sew the Step 4 triangle squares together in pairs; press. Sew the pairs together; press. Sew the 2-1/2 x 8-1/2-inch **EGGPLANT** rectangle to the bottom edge of this unit; press. *At this point the unit should measure 8-1/2 x 10-1/2-inches.*

Make 1

Step 6 ✎ Sew the 2-1/2 x 10-1/2-inch **BEIGE** and **EGGPLANT** rectangles together in pairs; press. Sew the pairs to both side edges of the Step 5 unit; press. Sew the Step 3 roof unit to the top edge of this unit; press. *At this point the house unit should measure 16-1/2-inches square.*

Make 1

145

(continued on the next page)

Step 7 ✌ With right sides together, layer together the 2-7/8 x 14-inch **DARK GREEN** strip and 1 of the 2-7/8 x 14-inch **BEIGE** strips. Press together, but do not sew. Cut the layered strips into squares. Cut each layered square in half diagonally to make 8 sets of layered triangles. Stitch 1/4-inch from the diagonal edge of each pair of triangles; press. *At this point each triangle-pieced square should measure 2-1/2-inches square.*

Crosscut
4, 2-7/8-inch squares

Make 8, 2-1/2-inch
triangle-pieced squares

Step 8 ✌ Sew a 2-1/2-inch **PLUM #2** square to the right edge of a Step 7 triangle-pieced square; press. Make 8 units. Sew the units together; press. *At this point the strip should measure 4-1/2 x 16-1/2-inches.*

Make 8

Step 9 ✌ Repeat the process in Step 7 using the 2-7/8 x 14-inch **MEDIUM GREEN** strip and the remaining 2-7/8 x 14-inch **BEIGE** strip to make 8 triangle-pieced squares. Sew a 2-1/2-inch **BRICK #2** square to the

Make 1

right edge of a triangle-pieced square; press. Make 8 units. Sew the units together; press. *At this point the strip should measure 4-1/2 x 16-1/2-inches.*

Make 8

Make 1

Step 10 ✌ Referring to the block diagram, sew the Step 9 strip to the bottom edge of the Step 6 house unit; press. Sew the 4-1/2-inch **DARK GREEN** square to the bottom edge of the Step 8 strip; press. Sew this strip to the left edge of the house unit; press. *At this point the block should measure 20-1/2-inches square.* Refer to **Appliqué the Birdhouse Holes** on page 150 for complete instructions on adding the birdhouse hole.

SAFE HAVEN Block 11

Safe Haven
Block - *Twelve*

Cutting

From BEIGE PRINT:
❋ Cut 1, 4-1/2 x 42-inch strip.
   From the strip cut:
     2, 4-1/2-inch squares
     2, 3-1/2 x 4-1/2-inch rectangles
     1, 2-1/2 x 4-1/2-inch rectangle
❋ Cut 12, 2-1/2-inch squares

From DARK GREEN PRINT:
❋ Cut 2, 2-1/2 x 8-1/2-inch rectangles
❋ Cut 2, 2-1/2-inch squares

From MEDIUM GREEN PRINT:
❋ Cut 3, 2-1/2 x 8-1/2-inch rectangles

From BROWN PRINT #1:
❋ Cut 1, 2-1/2 x 20-inch strip.
   From the strip cut:
     1, 2-1/2 x 4-1/2-inch rectangle
     4, 2-1/2-inch squares
     2, 1-1/2-inch squares

From RED PRINT #1:
❋ Cut 1, 4-1/2 x 8-1/2-inch rectangle

From DARK BLUE PRINT:
❋ Cut 1, 2-1/2 x 42-inch strip

From GOLD PRINT #1:
❋ Cut 1, 2-1/2 x 42-inch strip

From ROSE PRINT:
❋ Cut 4, 2-1/2 x 16-1/2-inch strips

Piecing

Step 1 ❧ With right sides together, position a 2-1/2-inch **DARK GREEN** square on the corner of the 2-1/2 x 4-1/2-inch **BEIGE** rectangle. Draw a diagonal line on the square; stitch, trim, and press. Repeat this process at the opposite corner of the rectangle. Sew 2-1/2-inch **BEIGE** squares to both side edges of this unit; press. *At this point the unit should measure 2-1/2 x 8-1/2-inches.*

Make 1

Step 2 ❧ With right sides together, position 2-1/2-inch **BEIGE** squares on the corners of a 2-1/2 x 8-1/2-inch **DARK GREEN** rectangle. Draw a diagonal line on the squares; stitch, trim, and press.

Make 2

(continued on the next page)

147

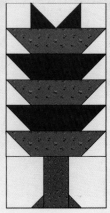

Step 3 ✌ Repeat the process in Step 2 using 2-1/2-inch **BEIGE** squares and a 2-1/2 x 8-1/2-inch **MEDIUM GREEN** rectangle.

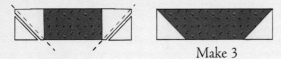

Make 3

Step 4 ✌ With right sides together, position a 1-1/2-inch **BROWN #1** square on the lower right corner of a 3-1/2 x 4-1/2-inch **BEIGE** rectangle. Draw a diagonal line on the square; stitch, trim, and press. Repeat this process positioning the **BROWN #1** square on the lower left corner of the remaining **BEIGE** rectangle.

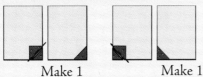

Make 1   Make 1

Step 5 ✌ Sew the Step 4 units to both side edges of the 2-1/2 x 4-1/2-inch **BROWN #1** rectangle to complete the trunk unit; press. *At this point the trunk unit should measure 4-1/2 x 8-1/2-inches.*

Make 1

Step 6 ✌ Sew the Step 1, 2, and 3 units together; press. Sew the Step 5 trunk

unit to the bottom edge of this unit; press. *At this point the tree unit should measure 8-1/2 x 16-1/2-inches.*

Make 1

Step 7 ✌ With right sides together, position a 4-1/2-inch **BEIGE** square on the corner of the 4-1/2 x 8-1/2-inch **RED #1** rectangle. Draw a diagonal line on the square; stitch, trim, and press. Repeat this process at the opposite corner of the rectangle. *At this point the roof unit should measure 4-1/2 x 8-1/2-inches.*

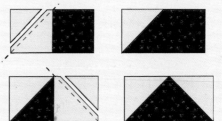

Make 1

Step 8 ✌ Aligning long edges, sew the 2-1/2 x 42-inch **DARK BLUE** and **GOLD #1** strips together; press. Cut the strip set into segments. Sew 3 of the

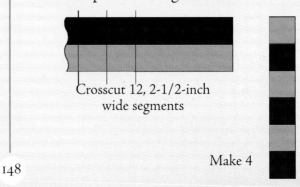

Crosscut 12, 2-1/2-inch wide segments

Make 4

segments together end to end; press. Make 4 strips. *At this point each strip should measure 2-1/2 x 12-1/2-inches.*

Step 9 ✐ Sew the Step 8 strips together, alternating the colors; press. Sew the Step 7 roof unit to the top edge of this unit; press. *At this point the house unit should measure 8-1/2 x 16-1/2-inches.*

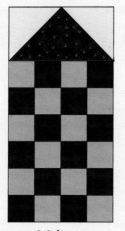

Make 1

Step 10 ✐ Referring to the block diagram, sew the Step 6 tree unit to the left edge of the Step 9 house unit; press.

Step 11 ✐ Sew 2-1/2 x 16-1/2-inch **ROSE** strips to the top/bottom edges of the house/tree unit; press. Add 2-1/2-inch **BROWN #1** squares to both ends of the remaining 2-1/2 x 16-1/2-inch **ROSE** strips; press. Sew the strips to the side edges of the unit; press. *At this point the block should measure 20-1/2-inches square.* Refer to **Appliqué the Birdhouse Holes** on page 150 for complete instructions on adding the birdhouse holes.

SAFE HAVEN Block 12

149

Appliqué the Birdhouse Holes

Step 1 ✎ Make a lightweight cardboard template using the birdhouse hole pattern below.

Birdhouse Hole Template

Step 2 ✎ Position the template on the wrong side of the fabric chosen for the appliqué and trace around the template, adding a 3/4-inch margin around each shape. Remove the template and cut a scant 1/4-inch beyond the drawn lines.

Step 3 ✎ To create smooth, round circles, run a line of basting stitches around each circle, placing the stitches halfway between the drawn line and the cut edge

of the circle. After basting, keep the needle and thread attached for the next step.

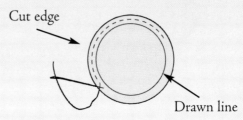

Cut edge

Drawn line

Step 4 ✎ Place the cardboard template on the wrong side of the fabric circle and tug on the basting stitches, gathering the fabric over the template. When the thread is tight, space the gathers evenly, and make a knot to secure the thread. Clip the thread, press the circle, and remove the cardboard template. Continue this process to make 21 birdhouse holes.

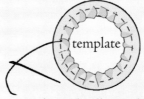

template

Make 21 birdhouse holes

Step 5 ✎ Hand appliqué the birdhouse holes to the blocks with matching thread.

Finishing the Quilt

Quilt Center

Cutting

From LARGE GOLD FLORAL:
❋ Cut 5, 5-1/2 x 42-inch wide lattice strips

From EGGPLANT PRINT:
❋ Cut 9, 1-1/2 x 42-inch narrow lattice strips

Quilt Center Assembly

Step 1 ❧ Referring to the quilt diagram for block placement, sew the blocks together in 3 vertical rows of 4 blocks each; press. *At this point the 2 outer block rows should measure 20-1/2 x 80-1/2-inches. The middle block row should measure 18-1/2 x 80-1/2-inches.*

Step 2 ❧ Diagonally piece the 5-1/2-inch wide **LARGE GOLD FLORAL** lattice strips. Cut 2, 5-1/2 x 80-1/2-inch lattice strips (or the length of your block rows).

Step 3 ❧ Diagonally piece the 1-1/2-inch wide **EGGPLANT** lattice strips. Cut 4, 1-1/2 x 80-1/2-inch lattice strips (or the length of your block rows).

Step 4 ❧ Sew the 1-1/2-inch wide **EGGPLANT** lattice strips to both side edges of the 5-1/2-inch wide **LARGE GOLD FLORAL** lattice strips; press. Sew together the pieced lattice strips and the block rows; press.

Borders

NOTE: *The yardage given allows for the border strips to be cut on the crosswise grain. Diagonally piece the strips as needed, referring to **Diagonal Piecing** instructions on page 253. Read through **Border** instructions on page 250, for general instructions on adding borders.*

Cutting

From EGGPLANT PRINT:
❋ Cut 8, 1-1/2 x 42-inch inner border strips

From GOLD PRINT #1:
❋ Cut 8, 1-1/2 x 42-inch first middle border strips

From BRICK PRINT #2:
❋ Cut 9, 1-1/2 x 42-inch second middle border strips

From LARGE GOLD FLORAL:
❋ Cut 11, 5-1/2 x 42-inch outer border strips

Attaching the Borders

Step 1 ❧ Attach the 1-1/2-inch wide **EGGPLANT** inner border strips.

Step 2 ❧ Attach the 1-1/2-inch wide **GOLD #1** first middle border strips.

Step 3 ❧ Attach the 1-1/2-inch wide **BRICK #2** second middle border strips.

Step 4 ❧ Attach the 5-1/2-inch wide **LARGE GOLD FLORAL** outer border strips.

Putting It All Together

❋ Cut the 8 yard length of backing fabric in thirds crosswise to make 3, 2-2/3 yard lengths. Refer to **Quilting the Project** on page 252 for complete instructions.

Binding

From BLUE DIAGONAL CHECK:
❋ Cut 10, 2-3/4 x 42-inch strips

Sew the binding to the quilt using a 3/8-inch seam allowance. This measurement will produce a 1/2-inch wide finished binding. Refer to **Binding** and **Diagonal Piecing** on page 253 for complete instructions.

A QUILTER'S GARDEN™

*Share a gardener's delight in the color and fragrance
of spring with this beautiful quilt.*

As many of my readers know, I am an avid gardener. I enjoy pouring over
seed catalogs in the winter and, as I look at individual flowers, I imagine
them as geometric patterns. There is nothing better after a Minnesota winter
than to get into the garden and enjoy the warm days of spring.
Designing this quilt was especially fun for this gardener, and many of my
favorite flowers are included as individual blocks, including
Painted Daisy, Tulips, Verbena and Fan Flower. You will see
these growing in my yard!
Very often, flowers are appliquéd on quilts. A QUILTER'S GARDEN
takes a different approach with these pieced blocks.
The blocks are set on point, with alternating plain blocks, offering many
opportunities for creative quilting. The finished quilt is reminiscent of an
antique quilt. It has traditional appeal, but uses today's quick techniques.
I really enjoyed designing these blocks and hope you will enjoy making
your very own quilted garden.

A QUILTER'S GARDEN

—✂—

81 x 98-inches

Fabrics & Supplies

1-7/8 yards
BEIGE PRINT
for all 12 blocks

1/4 yard
MEDIUM GOLD PRINT
for blocks 1, 5

1/4 yard
LIGHT BLUE PRINT
for blocks 1,12

5/8 yard
MEDIUM GREEN PRINT
for blocks 1, 2, 5, 7, 8, 9, 11

1/4 yard
PLUM PRINT #1
for blocks 1, 3, 12

1/4 yard
RED FLORAL
for blocks 2, 6, 7

1/4 yard
PINK PRINT
for blocks 1, 3, 6, 11

1/2 yard
GOLD FLORAL
for blocks 2, 5, 6, 7, 8, 9, 11

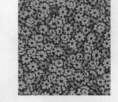

1/4 yard
LIGHT GOLD PRINT
for blocks 2, 10, 12

1/4 yard
RED DIAGONAL CHECK
for blocks 4, 8

1/2 yard
**GREEN DIAGONAL
CHECK** for blocks 2, 7, 9, 10

3/8 yard
DARK BLUE PRINT
for blocks 5, 8, 10, 11

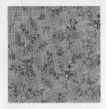

1 yard **LIGHT GREEN
PRINT** for blocks 3, 4, 6, 12,
first middle border

7/8 yard
LIGHT GREEN FLORAL
for alternate blocks

1-1/8 yards **PLUM PRINT #2**
for blocks 3, 4, 9,
inner/third middle borders

1-1/4 yards
BEIGE FLORAL
for side and corner triangles

3/8 yard
RED PRINT
for blocks 4, 5, 10

3-1/8 yards **LARGE
MULTICOLOR FLORAL**
for third middle/outer borders

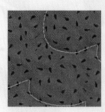 7/8 yard
MEDIUM GREEN PRINT
for binding

 7-1/8 yards backing fabric
quilt batting,
at least 85 x 102-inches

Before beginning this project, read through **Getting Started** on page 244.

*This fabric key should be used as a helpful guideline in selecting fabric for your quilt project.
We cannot guarantee that a specific fabric will be available at your favorite quilt store,
but suitable substitutions can be found.*

A Quilter's Garden
Block 1 - *Bachelor Buttons*

Cutting

From BEIGE PRINT:
❋ Cut 1, 4-1/4-inch square for stem unit
❋ Cut 1, 2-7/8 x 30-inch strip
❋ Cut 1, 1-1/2 x 42-inch strip.
  From the strip cut:
    16, 1-1/2-inch squares

From LIGHT BLUE PRINT:
❋ Cut 1, 2-1/2 x 42-inch strip.
  From the strip cut:
    8, 2-1/2-inch squares

From PLUM PRINT #1:
❋ Cut 4, 2-1/2-inch squares

From PINK PRINT:
❋ Cut 4, 2-1/2-inch squares

From MEDIUM GOLD PRINT:
❋ Cut 1, 1-1/2 x 42-inch strip.
  From the strip cut:
    16, 1-1/2-inch squares

From MEDIUM GREEN PRINT:
❋ Cut 1, 2-7/8 x 30-inch strip
❋ Cut 1, 1-1/2 x 7-inch strip for stem unit

Piecing

Step 1 ✍ With right sides together, position a 1-1/2-inch **BEIGE** square on the upper left corner of a 2-1/2-inch **LIGHT BLUE** square. Draw a diagonal line on the **BEIGE** square, and stitch on the line. Trim the seam allowance to 1/4-inch; press. Position a 1-1/2-inch **MEDIUM GOLD** square on the lower right corner of the **LIGHT BLUE** square. Draw a diagonal line on the **GOLD** square; stitch, trim, and press. *At this point each unit should measure 2-1/2-inches square.*

 Make 8

Step 2 ✍ Sew the Step 1 units together in pairs; press. Sew the pairs together to make the flower blocks; press. *At this point each flower block should measure 4-1/2-inches square.*

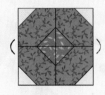 Make 2

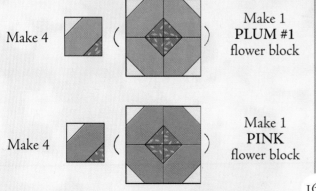

Step 3 ✔ Repeat Step 1 using a 1-1/2-inch **BEIGE** square, a 1-1/2-inch **MEDIUM GOLD** square, and a 2-1/2-inch **PLUM #1** square. Sew the units together in pairs; press. Sew the pairs together to make a flower block; press. Repeat this process using a 1-1/2-inch **BEIGE** square, a 1-1/2-inch **MEDIUM GOLD** square, and a 2-1/2-inch **PINK** square. Sew the units together in pairs; press. Sew the pairs together to make a flower block; press. *At this point each flower block should measure 4-1/2-inches square.*

Step 4 ✔ With right sides together, layer the 2-7/8 x 30-inch **MEDIUM GREEN** and **BEIGE** strips. Press together, but do not sew. Cut the layered strip into 8 squares. Cut the squares in half diagonally to make 16 sets of layered triangles. Stitch 1/4-inch from the diagonal edge of each pair of triangles; press. *At this point each triangle-pieced square should measure 2-1/2-inches square.*

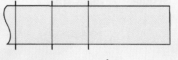

Crosscut 8, 2-7/8-inch squares

Make 16, 2-1/2-inch triangle-pieced squares

Make 4 ( ) Make 1 **PLUM #1** flower block

Make 4 ( ) Make 1 **PINK** flower block

(continued on the next page)

161

Step 5 ✎ Sew the Step 4 triangle-pieced squares together in pairs; press. Sew the pairs together to make the pinwheel blocks; press. *At this point each pinwheel block should measure 4-1/2-inches square.*

Make 8

Make 4

Step 6 ✎ To make the stem unit, cut the 4-1/4-inch **BEIGE** square in half diagonally to make 2 triangles. Center a **BEIGE** triangle on the 1-1/2 x 7-inch **MEDIUM GREEN** strip; stitch. Center the remaining **BEIGE** triangle on the **MEDIUM GREEN** strip; stitch, and press. Trim the stem unit so it measures 4-1/2-inches square.

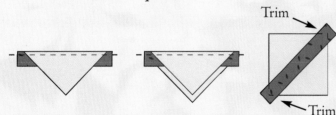

Step 7 ✎ Sew the Step 2, Step 3, Step 5, and Step 6 units together in 3 vertical rows; press. Sew the vertical rows together; press. *At this point the block should measure 12-1/2-inches square.*

A QUILTER'S GARDEN Block 1

A QUILTER'S GARDEN
BLOCK 2- *Star Gazer*

CUTTING

From BEIGE PRINT:
❋ Cut 1, 2-7/8-inch square
❋ Cut 1, 2-1/2 x 30-inch strip.
   From the strip cut:
      2, 2-1/2 x 4-1/2-inch rectangles
      6, 2-1/2-inch squares

From RED FLORAL:
❋ Cut 8, 2-1/2-inch squares

From GOLD FLORAL:
❋ Cut 1, 2-7/8 x 42-inch strip.
   From the strip cut:
      1, 2-7/8-inch square
      3, 2-1/2 x 4-1/2-inch rectangles
      4, 2-1/2-inch squares

From LIGHT GOLD PRINT:
❋ Cut 1, 4-1/2-inch square

From GREEN DIAGONAL CHECK:
❋ Cut 1, 2-1/2 x 42-inch strip.
   From the strip cut:
      4, 2-1/2 x 4-1/2-inch rectangles
      2, 2-1/2-inch squares

From MEDIUM GREEN PRINT:
❋ Cut 1, 2-1/2 x 42-inch strip.
   From the strip cut:
      2, 2-1/2 x 10-1/2-inch rectangles

PIECING

Step 1 ↝ With right sides together, layer the 2-7/8-inch **GOLD FLORAL** and **BEIGE** squares. Press together, but do not sew. Cut the layered square in half diagonally. Stitch 1/4-inch from the diagonal edge of one pair of triangles; press. Sew a 2-1/2-inch **BEIGE** square to the left edge of the triangle-pieced square; press. *At this point the unit should measure 2-1/2 x 4-1/2-inches.*

Make 1, 2-1/2-inch
triangle-pieced square

Make 1

Step 2 ↝ With right sides together, position a 2-1/2-inch **BEIGE** square on the left corner of the 2-1/2 x 4-1/2-inch **GOLD FLORAL** rectangle. Draw a diagonal line on the square; stitch, trim, and press. Sew the Step 1 unit to the top edge of this unit; press. *At this point the unit should measure 4-1/2-inches square.*

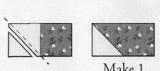

Make 1   Make 1

(continued on the next page)

Step 3 ❧ With right sides together, position a 2-1/2-inch **GOLD FLORAL** square on the corner of a 2-1/2 x 4-1/2-inch **BEIGE** rectangle. Draw a diagonal line on the square; stitch, trim, and press. Repeat this process at the opposite corner of the rectangle. *At this point each unit should measure 2-1/2 x 4-1/2-inches.*

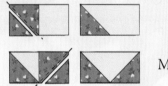

Make 2

Step 4 ❧ Repeat Step 3 using 4 of the 2-1/2-inch **RED FLORAL** squares and the 2-1/2 x 4-1/2-inch **GOLD FLORAL** rectangles. Sew the Step 3 units to the top edge of the units; press. *At this point each unit should measure 4-1/2-inches square.*

Make 2

Make 2

Step 5 ❧ Repeat Step 3 using 4 of the 2-1/2-inch **RED FLORAL** squares and 2 of the 2-1/2 x 4-1/2-inch **GREEN DIAGONAL CHECK** rectangles. Referring to the block diagram, sew one of the units to the bottom edge of the 4-1/2-inch **LIGHT GOLD** square and sew a Step 4 unit to the top edge of the **LIGHT GOLD** square; press.

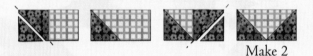

Make 2

Step 6 ❧ With right sides together, position a 2-1/2-inch **BEIGE** square on the right corner of a 2-1/2 x 4-1/2-inch **GREEN DIAGONAL CHECK** rectangle. Draw a diagonal line on the square; stitch, trim, and press. Repeat this process to make another unit, but change the direction of the drawn line. *At this point each unit should measure 2-1/2 x 4-1/2-inches.*

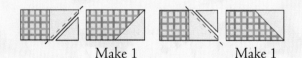

Make 1

Make 1

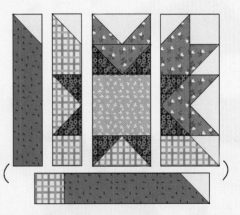

Step 7 ✒ With right sides together, position a 2-1/2-inch **BEIGE** square on the right corner of a 2-1/2 x 10-1/2-inch **MEDIUM GREEN** rectangle. Draw a diagonal line on the square; stitch, trim, and press. Repeat this process to make another unit, but change the direction of the drawn line. *At this point each unit should measure 2-1/2 x 10-1/2-inches.*

Make 1 leaf A unit

Make 1 leaf B unit

Step 8 ✒ Sew a 2-1/2-inch **GREEN DIAGONAL CHECK** square to the left edge of the leaf B unit; press.

Step 9 ✒ Sew the Step 2, Step 5, Step 6, and Step 7 units together in 4 vertical rows; press. Sew the rows together; press. Sew the Step 8 leaf B unit to the bottom edge of this unit; press. *At this point the block should measure 12-1/2-inches square.*

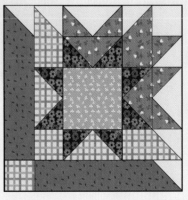

A QUILTER'S GARDEN Block 2

A Quilter's Garden
Block 3 - *Bleeding Heart*

Cutting

From BEIGE PRINT:
❋ Cut 1, 4-1/4-inch square for stem unit
❋ Cut 1, 2-1/2 x 35-inch strip.
  From the strip cut:
    4, 2-1/2-inch squares
    16, 1-1/2-inch squares
❋ Cut 1, 1 x 35-inch strip.
  From the strip cut:
    32, 1-inch squares

From PLUM PRINT #1:
❋ Cut 8, 2-1/2-inch squares

From PLUM PRINT #2:
❋ Cut 4, 2-1/2-inch squares

From PINK PRINT:
❋ Cut 8, 2-1/2-inch squares

From LIGHT GREEN PRINT:
❋ Cut 1, 2-1/2 x 42-inch strip.
  From the strip cut:
    8, 2-1/2-inch squares
    1, 1-1/2 x 7-inch strip for stem unit

Piecing

Step 1 ✑ With right sides together, position a 1-inch **BEIGE** square on the upper corners of a 2-1/2-inch **PLUM #1** square. Draw a diagonal line on the **BEIGE** squares; stitch, trim, and press. *At this point each unit should measure 2-1/2-inches square.*

  Make 8

Step 2 ✑ With right sides together, position a 1-inch **BEIGE** square on the upper corners of a 2-1/2-inch **PINK** square. Draw a diagonal line on the **BEIGE** squares; stitch, trim, and press. *At this point each unit should measure 2-1/2-inches square.*

 Make 8

Step 3 ✑ With right sides together, position a 1-1/2-inch **BEIGE** square on the upper right and lower left corners of a 2-1/2-inch **LIGHT GREEN** square. Draw a diagonal line on the **BEIGE** squares; stitch, trim, and press. *At this point each unit should measure 2-1/2-inches square.*

  Make 8

Step 4 ✒ Referring to the diagram for placement, sew a **PLUM #1** Step 1) Make 4 unit to the right edge of a Step 3 unit; press. Sew a **PLUM #1** Step 1 unit to the left edge of a 2-1/2-inch **PLUM #2** square; press. Sew the 2 units together; press. *At this point each unit should measure 4-1/2-inches square.*

Step 5 ✒ Referring to the diagram for placement, sew a **PINK** Step 2 unit to) Make 4 the right edge of a Step 3 unit; press. Sew a **PINK** Step 2 unit to the left edge of a 2-1/2-inch **BEIGE** square; press. Sew the 2 units together; press. *At this point each unit should measure 4-1/2-inches square.*

Step 6 ✒ To make the stem unit, cut the 4-1/4-inch **BEIGE** square in half diagonally to make 2 triangles. Center a **BEIGE** triangle on the 1-1/2 x 7-inch **LIGHT GREEN** strip; stitch. Center the remaining **BEIGE** triangle on the **LIGHT GREEN** strip; stitch, and press. Trim the stem unit so it measures 4-1/2-inches square.

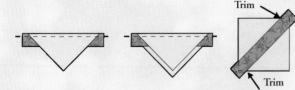

Step 7 ✒ Sew the Step 4, Step 5, and Step 6 units together in 3 vertical rows; press. Sew the rows together; press. *At this point the block should measure 12-1/2-inches square.*

A QUILTER'S GARDEN Block 3

A QUILTER'S GARDEN
BLOCK 4 - *Cactus Flower*

CUTTING

From BEIGE PRINT:
❋ Cut 1, 2-7/8 x 42-inch strip.
  From the strip cut:
    1, 2-7/8-inch square
    2, 2-1/2 x 6-1/2-inch rectangles
    2, 2-1/2 x 4-1/2-inch rectangles
❋ Cut 1, 2-1/2 x 42-inch strip.
  From the strip cut:
    8, 2-1/2-inch squares

From LIGHT GREEN PRINT:
❋ Cut 1, 2-1/2 x 42-inch strip.
  From the strip cut:
    2, 2-1/2 x 6-1/2-inch rectangles
    2, 2-1/2 x 4-1/2-inch rectangles
    2, 2-1/2-inch squares

From RED PRINT:
❋ Cut 2, 2-1/2 x 6-1/2-inch rectangles

From PLUM PRINT #2:
❋ Cut 3, 2-1/2-inch squares

From RED DIAGONAL PRINT:
❋ Cut 1, 2-7/8 x 42-inch strip.
  From the strip cut:
    1, 2-7/8-inch square
    1, 2-1/2 x 6-1/2-inch rectangle
    1, 2-1/2 x 4-1/2-inch rectangle

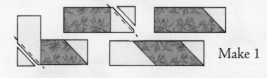

Piecing

Step 1 ✒ With right sides together, position a 2-1/2-inch **BEIGE** square on the right corner of a 2-1/2 x 6-1/2-inch **LIGHT GREEN** rectangle. Draw a diagonal line on the square; stitch, trim, and press. Position a 2-1/2 x 4-1/2-inch **BEIGE** rectangle on the left corner of the **LIGHT GREEN** rectangle. Draw a diagonal line on the **BEIGE** rectangle; stitch, trim, and press. *At this point the unit should measure 2-1/2 x 8-1/2-inches.*

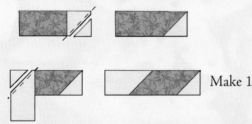

Make 1

Step 2 ✒ Position a 2-1/2 x 6-1/2-inch **BEIGE** rectangle on the right corner of a 2-1/2 x 4-1/2-inch **LIGHT GREEN** rectangle. Draw a diagonal line on the **BEIGE** rectangle; stitch, trim, and press. *At this point the unit should measure 2-1/2 x 8-1/2-inches.*

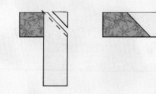

Make 1

Step 3 ✒ Sew the Step 2 unit to the top edge of the Step 1 unit; press. *At this point the unit should measure 4-1/2 x 8-1/2-inches.*

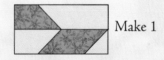

Make 1

Step 4 ✒ Position a 2-1/2-inch **BEIGE** square on the right corner of a 2-1/2 x 6-1/2-inch **LIGHT GREEN** rectangle. Draw a diagonal line on the square; stitch, trim, and press. Position a 2-1/2 x 4-1/2-inch **BEIGE** rectangle on the left corner of the **LIGHT GREEN** rectangle. Draw a diagonal line on the **BEIGE** rectangle; stitch, trim, and press. *At this point the unit should measure 2-1/2 x 8-1/2-inches.*

Make 1

169

(continued on the next page)

Step 5 ❧ Position a 2-1/2 x 6-1/2-inch **BEIGE** rectangle on the right corner of a 2-1/2 x 4-1/2-inch **LIGHT GREEN** rectangle. Draw a diagonal line on the **BEIGE** rectangle; stitch, trim, and press. *At this point the unit should measure 2-1/2 x 8-1/2-inches.*

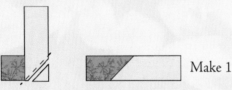

Make 1

Step 6 ❧ Sew the Step 4 unit to the top edge of the Step 5 unit; press. *At this point the unit should measure 4-1/2 x 8-1/2-inches.*

Make 1

Step 7 ❧ Sew the 2-1/2-inch **LIGHT GREEN** and **BEIGE** squares together in pairs; press. Sew the pairs together to make a four-patch unit; press. Sew the four-patch unit to the bottom edge of the Step 6 unit; press. *At this point the unit should measure 4-1/2 x 12-1/2-inches.*

Make 1

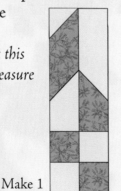

Make 1

Step 8 ❧ Position a 2-1/2-inch **BEIGE** square on the right corner of a 2-1/2 x 6-1/2-inch **RED** rectangle. Draw a diagonal line on the square; stitch, trim, and press. Sew a 2-1/2-inch **PLUM** #2 square to the left edge of this unit; press. Sew this unit to the top of the Step 3 unit; press. *At this point the unit should measure 6-1/2 x 8-1/2-inches.*

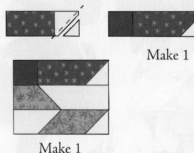

Make 1

Make 1

Step 9 ❧ Position a 2-1/2-inch **BEIGE** square on the right corner of a 2-1/2 x 6-1/2-inch **RED** rectangle. Draw a diagonal line on the square; stitch, trim, and press. Repeat this process using a 2-1/2-inch **BEIGE** square and a 2-1/2 x 6-1/2-inch **RED DIAGONAL CHECK** rectangle. Notice the direction of the drawn line; trim and press. *At this point each unit should measure 2-1/2 x 6-1/2-inches.*

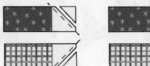

Make 1

Make 1

Step 10 ✍ Position a 2-1/2-inch **BEIGE** square on the right corner of a 2-1/2 x 4-1/2-inch **RED DIAGONAL CHECK** rectangle. Draw a diagonal line on the square; stitch, trim, and press. *At this point the unit should measure 2-1/2 x 4-1/2-inches.*

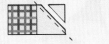 Make 1

Step 11 ✍ With right sides together, layer the 2-7/8-inch **BEIGE** and **RED DIAGONAL CHECK** squares. Press together, but do not sew. Cut the layered square in half diagonally to make 2 sets of layered triangles. Stitch 1/4-inch from the diagonal edge of each pair of triangles; press. *At this point each triangle-pieced square should measure 2-1/2-inches square.*

 Make 2, 2-1/2-inch triangle-pieced squares

Step 12 ✍ Referring to the block diagram, sew the triangle-pieced squares and 2-1/2-inch **PLUM #2** squares together in pairs; press. Sew the pairs together to make a four-patch unit; press.

Step 13 ✍ Sew the units together in 2 vertical rows; press. Sew the rows together; press. *At this point the block should measure 12-1/2-inches square.*

A QUILTER'S GARDEN Block 4

A QUILTER'S GARDEN
BLOCK 5 - *Lollipop Lily*

CUTTING

From BEIGE PRINT:
❊ Cut 1, 6-1/4-inch square for stem unit
❊ Cut 1, 2 x 33-inch strip.
   From the strip cut:
     6, 2 x 3-1/2-inch rectangles
❊ Cut 1, 1-1/2 x 33-inch strip.
   From the strip cut:
     12, 1-1/2-inch squares

From MEDIUM GOLD PRINT:
❊ Cut 1, 3-1/2-inch square
❊ Cut 15, 1-1/2-inch squares

From RED PRINT:
❊ Cut 4, 2 x 3-1/2-inch rectangles
❊ Cut 8, 2-inch squares

From DARK BLUE PRINT:
❊ Cut 2, 2 x 3-1/2-inch rectangles
❊ Cut 4, 2-inch squares

From GOLD FLORAL:
❊ Cut 2, 3-1/2-inch squares

From MEDIUM GREEN PRINT:
❊ Cut 1, 4-1/2-inch square
❊ Cut 1, 1-1/2 x 9-1/2-inch strip
   for stem unit

PIECING

Step 1 ✎ Sew 1-1/2-inch **MEDIUM GOLD** squares to both sides of a 1-1/2-inch **BEIGE** square; press.

 Make 6

Step 2 ✎ Sew 1-1/2-inch **BEIGE** squares to both sides of a 1-1/2-inch **MEDIUM GOLD** square; press.

Make 3

Step 3 ✎ Sew the Step 1 units to the top and bottom edges of the Step 2 units; press. *At this point each nine-patch block should measure 3-1/2-inches square.*

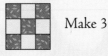 Make 3

Step 4 ✎ Position a 2-inch **RED** square on the corner of a 2 x 3-1/2-inch **BEIGE** rectangle. Draw a diagonal line on the square; stitch, trim, and press. Repeat this process at the opposite corner of the rectangle. Sew a 2 x 3-1/2-inch **RED** rectangle to the bottom edge of each unit; press.

 Make 4

Step 5 Repeat Step 4 using 2-inch **DARK BLUE** squares and a 2 x 3-1/2-inch **BEIGE** rectangle. Sew a 2 x 3-1/2-inch **DARK BLUE** rectangle to the bottom edge of the unit; press.

 Make 2

Step 6 Sew a nine-patch block to the right edge of 2 of the **RED** Step 4 units, and to the right edge of 1 of the **DARK BLUE** Step 5 units; press. *At this point each unit should measure 3-1/2 x 6-1/2-inches.*

Make 1

Make 1

Step 7 Sew a 3-1/2-inch **GOLD FLORAL** square to the bottom edge of 2 of the Step 4 units; press. Sew a Step 6 **RED**/nine-patch unit to the left edge of each of these units; press. Sew a 3-1/2-inch **MEDIUM GOLD** square to the bottom edge of 1 of the **DARK BLUE** Step 5 units; press. Sew a Step 6 **DARK BLUE**/nine-patch unit to the left edge of this unit; press. *At this point each unit should measure 6-1/2-inches square.*

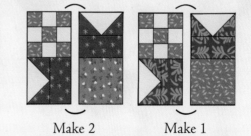

Make 2   Make 1

(continued on the next page)

Step 8 ✒ To make the stem unit, cut the 6-1/4-inch **BEIGE** square in half diagonally to make 2 triangles. Center a **BEIGE** triangle on the 1-1/2 x 9-1/2-inch **MEDIUM GREEN** strip; stitch. Center the remaining **BEIGE** triangle on the opposite edge of the **MEDIUM GREEN** strip; stitch and press. Trim the stem unit so it measures 6-1/2-inches square. Position the 4-1/2-inch **MEDIUM GREEN** square on the left corner of the stem unit, draw a diagonal line on the square; stitch, trim, and press. *At this point the stem unit should measure 6-1/2-inches square.*

Step 9 ✒ Sew the units together in 2 vertical rows; press. Sew the rows together; press. *At this point the block should measure 12-1/2-inches square.*

A QUILTER'S GARDEN Block 5

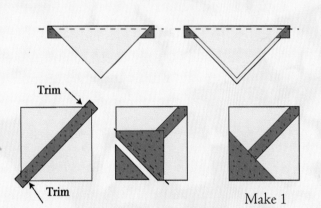

Trim

Trim

Make 1

A QUILTER'S GARDEN
BLOCK 6- *Painted Daisy*

CUTTING

From BEIGE PRINT:
❊ Cut 1, 1-1/2 x 42-inch strip.
  From the strip cut:
    8, 1-1/2-inch squares
    4, 1-1/2 x 3-1/2-inch rectangles
    4, 1-1/2 x 2-1/2-inch rectangles
❊ Cut 1, 2-1/2 x 42-inch strip.
  From the strip cut:
    8, 2-1/2-inch squares

From RED FLORAL:
❊ Cut 4, 2-1/2-inch squares

From LIGHT GREEN PRINT:
❊ Cut 4, 2-1/2 x 3-1/2-inch rectangles
❊ Cut 4, 2-1/2 -inch squares
❊ Cut 8, 1-1/2-inch squares

From GOLD FLORAL:
❊ Cut 5, 2-1/2-inch squares

From PINK PRINT:
❊ Cut 1, 2-1/2 x 42-inch strip.
  From the strip cut:
    8, 2-1/2 x 3-1/2-inch rectangles
    8, 1-1/2-inch squares

PIECING

Step 1 ✌ Position a 1-1/2-inch **LIGHT GREEN** square on the corner of a 2-1/2-inch **RED FLORAL** square. Draw a diagonal line on the **LIGHT GREEN** square; stitch, trim, and press. Repeat this process at the adjacent corner of the **RED FLORAL** square. *At this point each unit should measure 2-1/2-inches square.*

 Make 4

Step 2 ✌ Position a 1-1/2-inch **PINK** square on the corner of a 2-1/2-inch **LIGHT GREEN** square. Draw a diagonal line on the **PINK** square; stitch, trim, and press. Repeat this process at the opposite corner of the **LIGHT GREEN** square. *At this point each unit should measure 2-1/2-inches square.*

 Make 4

(continued on the next page)

175

Step 3 ❧ Sew Step 1 units to the top and bottom edges of a 2-1/2-inch **GOLD FLORAL** square; press. Sew Step 2 units to the side edges of the remaining Step 1 units; press. Sew these units to the side edges of the center strip; press. *At this point the unit should measure 6-1/2-inches square.*

Make 1

Step 4 ❧ Position a 1-1/2-inch **BEIGE** square on the corner of a 2-1/2 x 3-1/2-inch **LIGHT GREEN** rectangle. Draw a diagonal line on the square; stitch, trim, and press. Repeat this process at the adjacent corner of the rectangle. *At this point each unit should measure 2-1/2 x 3-1/2-inches.*

Make 4

Step 5 ❧ Position a 2-1/2-inch **BEIGE** square on the right corner of a 2-1/2 x 3-1/2-inch **PINK** rectangle. Draw a diagonal line on the square; stitch, trim, and press. Repeat with the remaining **PINK** rectangles, but change the direction of the drawn lines.

Make 4   Make 4

Step 6 ❧ Referring to the diagram for placement, sew the Step 5 units to both side edges of the Step 4 units; press. *At this point each unit should measure 3-1/2 x 6-1/2-inches.* Referring to the block diagram, sew 2 of the units to the top and bottom edges of the Step 3 unit; press.

Make 4

Step 7 ✏ Sew a 1-1/2 x 2-1/2-inch
BEIGE rectangle to the top edge of a
2-1/2-inch **GOLD FLORAL** square;
press. Sew a 1-1/2 x 3-1/2-inch **BEIGE**
rectangle to the left edge of this unit;
press. *At this point each unit should measure
3-1/2-inches square.*

  Make 4

Step 8 ✏ Sew the Step 7 units to both
side edges of the remaining Step 6 units;
press. Sew the 3 vertical rows together;
press. *At this point the block should measure
12-1/2-inches square.*

A QUILTER'S GARDEN Block 6

A QUILTER'S GARDEN
BLOCK 7 - *Windflower*

CUTTING

From BEIGE PRINT:

❊ Cut 1, 2-7/8 x 42-inch strip.
  From the strip cut:
    5, 2-7/8-inch squares
    2, 2-1/2 x 4-1/2-inch rectangles
    2, 2-1/2-inch squares

From RED FLORAL:

❊ Cut 1, 2-7/8 x 42-inch strip.
  From the strip cut:
    8, 2-7/8-inch squares

From GOLD FLORAL:

❊ Cut 1, 2-7/8 x 42-inch strip.
  From the strip cut:
    8, 2-7/8-inch squares

From GREEN DIAGONAL CHECK:

❊ Cut 1, 2-7/8-inch square
❊ Cut 1, 2-1/2 x 4-1/2-inch rectangle
❊ Cut 1, 2-1/2-inch square

From MEDIUM GREEN PRINT:

❊ Cut 1, 2-7/8 x 42-inch strip.
  From the strip cut:
    5, 2-7/8-inch squares
    1, 2-1/2 x 4-1/2-inch rectangle
    1, 2-1/2-inch square

PIECING

Step 1 ✌ With right sides together, layer the 2-7/8-inch **RED FLORAL** squares and the 2-7/8-inch **GOLD FLORAL** squares in pairs. Press together, but do not sew. Cut the layered squares in half diagonally to make 16 sets of layered triangles. Stitch 1/4-inch from the diagonal edge of each pair of triangles; press. *At this point each triangle-pieced square should measure 2-1/2-inches square.*

Make 16, 2-1/2-inch triangle-pieced squares

Step 2 ✌ Sew the triangle-pieced squares together in pairs; press. Sew the pairs together to make the pinwheel blocks. *At this point each pinwheel block should measure 4-1/2-inches square.*

Make 8

Make 4 RED FLORAL/GOLD FLORAL pinwheel blocks

Step 3 ❧ Repeat Step 1 layering 4 of the 2-7/8-inch **MEDIUM GREEN** squares and 4 of the 2-7/8-inch **BEIGE** squares in pairs. Make a total of 8, 2-1/2-inch triangle-pieced squares. Sew the triangle-pieced squares together in pairs; press. Sew the pairs together to make the pinwheel blocks. *At this point each pinwheel block should measure 4-1/2-inches square.*

Make 4

Make 2 **MEDIUM GREEN/BEIGE** pinwheel blocks

Step 4 ❧ Cut the remaining 2-7/8-inch **BEIGE, GREEN DIAGONAL CHECK,** and **MEDIUM GREEN** squares in half diagonally to make triangles. Sew together a **BEIGE** triangle and a **MEDIUM GREEN** triangle; press. Sew together a **BEIGE** triangle and a **GREEN DIAGONAL CHECK** triangle; press.

Make 1, 2-1/2-inch **MEDIUM GREEN/BEIGE** triangle-pieced square

Make 1, 2-1/2-inch **GREEN DIAGONAL CHECK/BEIGE** triangle-pieced square

Step 5 ❧ Sew the **GREEN DIAGONAL CHECK/BEIGE** triangle-pieced square to the top edge of the **MEDIUM GREEN/BEIGE** triangle-pieced square; press. Sew a 2-1/2 x 4-1/2-inch **BEIGE** rectangle to the right edge of this unit; press. *At this point the unit should measure 4-1/2-inches square.*

Make 1

Step 6 ❧ Position a 2-1/2-inch **BEIGE** square on the corner of the 2-1/2 x 4-1/2-inch **MEDIUM GREEN** rectangle. Draw a diagonal line on the square; stitch, trim, and press. *At this point the unit should measure 2-1/2 x 4-1/2-inches.*

Make 1

179

(continued on the next page)

Step 7 ✍ Repeat Step 6 using a 2-1/2-inch **BEIGE** square and the 2-1/2 x 4-1/2-inch **GREEN DIAGONAL CHECK** rectangle. Referring to the Step 8 diagram, sew this unit to the left edge of the Step 6 unit; press. Sew a 2-1/2 x 4-1/2-inch **BEIGE** rectangle to the top edge of this unit; press. *At this point the unit should measure 4-1/2 x 6-1/2 inches.*

 Make 1

Step 8 ✍ Sew the 2-1/2-inch **GREEN DIAGONAL CHECK** and **MEDIUM GREEN** squares together; press. Sew this unit to the bottom edge of the unit made in Step 7; press. *At this point the unit should measure 4-1/2 x 8-1/2-inches.*

Make 1

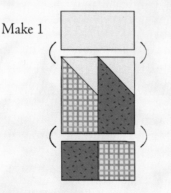

Step 9 ✍ Sew the pinwheel blocks and remaining units together in 3 vertical rows; press. Sew the rows together; press. *At this point the block should measure 12-1/2-inches square.*

A QUILTER'S GARDEN Block 7

A Quilter's Garden
Block 8 - *Zinnia*

Cutting

From BEIGE PRINT:
※ Cut 1, 2-7/8 x 42-inch strip.
   From the strip cut:
      6, 2-7/8-inch squares
      8, 2-1/2-inch squares

From DARK BLUE PRINT:
※ Cut 4, 2-1/2-inch squares

From GOLD FLORAL:
※ Cut 1, 4-1/2-inch square
※ Cut 4, 2-7/8-inch squares

From RED DIAGONAL CHECK:
※ Cut 1, 2-7/8 x 42-inch strip.
   From the strip cut:
      6, 2-7/8-inch squares
      4, 2-1/2 x 4-1/2-inch rectangles

From MEDIUM GREEN PRINT:
※ Cut 1, 2-1/2 x 42-inch strip.
   From the strip cut:
      4, 2-1/2 x 4-1/2-inch rectangles
      8, 2-1/2-inch squares

Piecing

Step 1 ↝ With right sides together, position a 2-1/2-inch **DARK BLUE** square on the upper left corner and the lower right corner of a 4-1/2-inch **GOLD FLORAL** square. Draw a diagonal line on the **DARK BLUE** squares; stitch, trim, and press. Repeat this process at the remaining corners of the **GOLD FLORAL** square. *At this point the unit should measure 4-1/2-inches square.*

Make 1

Step 2 ↝ WIth right sides together, position a 2-1/2-inch **MEDIUM GREEN** square on the corner of a 2-1/2 x 4-1/2-inch **RED DIAGONAL CHECK** rectangle. Draw a diagonal line on the square; stitch, trim, and press. Repeat this process at the opposite corner of the rectangle.

Make 4

181   *(continued on the next page)*

Step 3 ✒ With right sides together, layer 4 of the 2-7/8-inch **RED DIAGONAL CHECK** and **BEIGE** squares in pairs. Press together, but do not sew. Cut each square in half diagonally to make 8 sets of layered triangles. Stitch 1/4-inch from the diagonal edge of each pair of triangles; press. *At this point each triangle-pieced square should measure 2-1/2-inches square.*

Make 8, 2-1/2-inch
triangle-pieced squares

Step 4 ✒ With right sides together, position a Step 3 triangle-pieced square on the corner of a 2-1/2 x 4-1/2-inch **MEDIUM GREEN** rectangle (note the position of the seam line). Draw a diagonal line on the triangle-pieced square; stitch, trim, and press. Repeat this process at the opposite corner of the rectangle. *At this point the unit should measure 2-1/2 x 4-1/2-inches.*

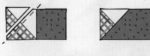

Make 4

Step 5 ✒ Sew the Step 4 units to the top edge of the Step 2 units; press. Referring to the block diagram, sew 2 of these units to the top and bottom edges of the Step 1 unit; press.

Make 4

Step 6 ✒ With right sides together, layer together 2 of the 2-7/8-inch **GOLD FLORAL** and **BEIGE** squares in pairs. Press together, but do not sew. Cut each square in half diagonally to make 4 sets of layered triangles. Stitch 1/4-inch from the diagonal edge of each pair of triangles; press. Sew a 2-1/2-inch **BEIGE** square to the right edge of the triangle-pieced squares; press. *At this point each unit should measure 2-1/2 x 4-1/2-inches.*

Make 4, 2-1/2-inch
triangle-pieced squares

Make 4

Step 7 ✍ With right sides together, layer 2 of the 2-7/8-inch **GOLD FLORAL** and **RED DIAGONAL CHECK** squares in pairs. Press together, but do not sew. Cut each square in half diagonally to make 4 sets of layered triangles. Stitch 1/4-inch from the diagonal edge of each pair of triangles; press. Sew a 2-1/2-inch **BEIGE** square to the left edge of the triangle-pieced squares; press. *At this point each unit should measure 2-1/2 x 4-1/2-inches.*

Make 4, 2-1/2-inch   Make 4
triangle-pieced squares

Step 8 ✍ Sew the Step 6 units to the top edge of the Step 7 units; press. *At this point each unit should measure 4-1/2-inches square.* Sew these units to the side edges of the remaining Step 5 units; press.

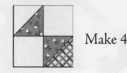 Make 4

Step 9 ✍ Sew the 3 vertical rows together; press. *At this point the block should measure 12-1/2-inches square.*

A QUILTER'S GARDEN BLOCK 8

183

A QUILTER'S GARDEN
BLOCK 9 - *Verbena*

CUTTING

From BEIGE PRINT:

❋ Cut 1, 4-1/4-inch square for stem unit

❋ Cut 1, 2-7/8 x 35-inch strip.
   From the strip cut:
   2, 2-7/8-inch squares
   11, 2-1/2-inch squares

From PLUM PRINT #2:

❋ Cut 1, 2-7/8-inch square

❋ Cut 4, 2-1/2 x 4-1/2-inch rectangles

From GREEN DIAGONAL CHECK:

❋ Cut 1, 2-7/8 x 42-inch strip.
   From the strip cut:
   1, 2-7/8-inch square
   5, 2-1/2 x 4-1/2-inch rectangles
   2, 2-1/2-inch squares

From MEDIUM GREEN PRINT:

❋ Cut 2, 2-1/2 x 4-1/2-inch rectangles

❋ Cut 2, 2-1/2-inch squares

❋ Cut 1, 1-1/2 x 7-inch strip for stem unit

From GOLD FLORAL:

❋ Cut 3, 2-1/2-inch squares

PIECING

Step 1 ✒ With right sides together, position a 2-1/2-inch **BEIGE** square on the right corner of a 2-1/2 x 4-1/2-inch **PLUM #2** rectangle. Draw a diagonal line on the square; stitch, trim, press. Repeat with the remaining rectangles, referring to the diagrams for the direction of the lines.

Make 3   Make 1

Step 2 ✒ With right sides together, position a 2-1/2-inch **BEIGE** square on the right corner of a 2-1/2 x 4-1/2-inch **GREEN DIAGONAL CHECK** rectangle. Draw a diagonal line on the square; stitch, trim, and press. Repeat with the remaining rectangles referring to the diagrams for the direction of the lines.

Make 3   Make 2

Step 3 ✒ Sew a Step 1 unit and a Step 2 unit together, referring to the diagrams for the direction of the seam lines and color placement.

Make 1   Make 1

Step 4 ✌ With right sides together, layer the 2-7/8-inch **PLUM #2** square and a 2-7/8-inch **BEIGE** square. Press together, but do not sew. Cut the layered square in half diagonally to make 2 sets of layered triangles. Stitch 1/4-inch from the diagonal edge of each pair of triangles; press. *At this point each triangle-pieced square should measure 2-1/2-inches square.* Repeat this process using the 2-7/8-inch **GREEN DIAGONAL CHECK** square and a 2-7/8-inch **BEIGE** square.

Make 2, 2-1/2-inch triangle-pieced squares, **PLUM #2/BEIGE**

Make 1, 2-1/2-inch triangle-pieced square, **GREEN DIAGONAL CHECK/BEIGE**

Step 5 ✌ Sew a 2-1/2-inch **GOLD FLORAL** square to the right edge of each of the Step 4 triangle-pieced squares; press. Referring to the diagrams, sew these units to the top edge of the corresponding Step 1 and Step 2 units; press. *At this point each unit should measure 4-1/2-inches square.*

Make 1   Make 1

Step 6 ✌ Sew a **PLUM #2** Step 5 unit to the left edge of the corresponding Step 3 unit; press. *At this point the unit should measure 4-1/2 x 8-1/2-inches.* Sew the remaining **PLUM #2** and **GREEN DIAGONAL CHECK** Step 5 units to

both sides of the corresponding Step 3 unit; press. *At this point the unit should measure 4-1/2 x 12-1/2-inches.*

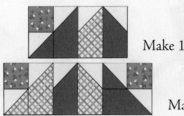

Make 1

Make 1

Step 7 ✌ With right sides together, position a 2-1/2-inch **BEIGE** square on the right corner of a 2-1/2 x 4-1/2-inch **MEDIUM GREEN** rectangle. Draw a line on the square; stitch, trim, and press. Repeat with the remaining rectangle, referring to the diagrams for the direction of the lines. Sew a 2-1/2-inch **GREEN DIAGONAL CHECK** square to the left edge of the unit shown at the right; press.

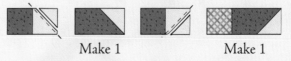

Make 1   Make 1

185

(continued on the next page)

Step 8 ❧ To make the stem unit, cut the 4-1/4-inch **BEIGE** square in half diagonally to make 2 triangles. Center a **BEIGE** triangle on the 1-1/2 x 7-inch **MEDIUM GREEN** strip; stitch. Center the remaining **BEIGE** triangle on the opposite edge of the **MEDIUM GREEN** strip; stitch and press. Trim the stem unit so it measures 4-1/2-inches square.

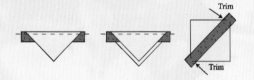

Step 9 ❧ Sew the Step 7 units to the Step 8 stem unit; press. *At this point the unit should measure 6-1/2-inches square.*

Make 1

Step 10 ❧ Sew 2-1/2-inch **MEDIUM GREEN** squares to the ends of the remaining Step 2 units; press. Referring to the diagram, sew the corresponding unit to the top of the Step 9 stem/leaf unit; press. Sew a 2-1/2-inch **GREEN DIAGONAL CHECK** square to the remaining unit; press. Sew this unit to the right edge of the stem/leaf unit;

press. *At this point the unit should measure 8-1/2-inches square.*

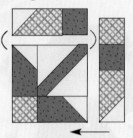

Step 11 ❧ Sew the units together in 2 vertical rows; press. Sew the rows together; press. *At this point the block should measure 12-1/2-inches square.*

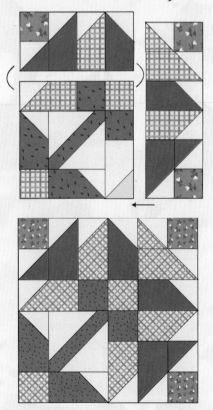

A QUILTER'S GARDEN Block 9

A QUILTER'S GARDEN
BLOCK 10 - *Fan Flower*

CUTTING

From BEIGE PRINT:
* ❊ Cut 1, 4-1/4-inch square for stem unit
* ❊ Cut 1, 2-7/8 x 35-1/2-inch strip.
  From the strip cut:
  6, 2-7/8-inch squares
  3, 2-1/2-inch squares
  2, 1-1/2 x 3-1/2-inch rectangles
  2, 1-1/2-inch squares

From RED PRINT:
* ❊ Cut 1, 2-7/8 x 42-inch strip.
  From the strip cut:
  6, 2-7/8-inch squares
  1, 2-1/2-inch square

From DARK BLUE PRINT:
* ❊ Cut 2, 2-1/2 x 4-1/2-inch rectangles
* ❊ Cut 2, 2-1/2-inch squares

From LIGHT GOLD PRINT:
* ❊ Cut 1, 2-1/2 x 4-1/2-inch rectangle
* ❊ Cut 1, 2-1/2-inch square

From GREEN DIAGONAL CHECK:
* ❊ Cut 2, 2-1/2-inch squares
* ❊ Cut 1, 1-1/2 x 7-inch strip for stem unit
* ❊ Cut 1, 1-1/2 x 6-1/2-inch rectangle
* ❊ Cut 2, 1-1/2 x 4-1/2-inch rectangles
* ❊ Cut 1, 1-1/2 x 2-1/2-inch rectangle

PIECING

Step 1 ❧ With right sides together, layer the 2-7/8-inch **RED** and **BEIGE** squares in pairs. Press together, but do not sew. Cut each square in half diagonally to make 12 sets of layered triangles. Stitch 1/4-inch from the diagonal edge of each pair of triangles; press. *At this point each triangle-pieced square should measure 2-1/2-inches square.*

 Make 12, 2-1/2-inch triangle-pieced squares

Step 2 ❧ Referring to the diagrams, sew the triangle-pieced squares together in pairs to make A units and B units; press. Add a 2-1/2-inch **BEIGE** square to the right edge of each B unit; press.

Make 3 triangle-pieced square A units

Make 3 triangle-pieced square B units

(continued on the next page)

Step 3 ✎ Sew a 2-1/2-inch **DARK BLUE** and **GREEN DIAGONAL CHECK** square together; press. Add a 2-1/2 x 4-1/2-inch **DARK BLUE** rectangle to the top edge of the unit; press. Sew an A unit to the top edge of the flower unit; press. Add a B unit to the left edge of the flower unit; press. *At this point each flower unit should measure 6-1/2-inches square.*

Make 2

Step 4 ✎ Sew the 2-1/2-inch **RED** and **LIGHT GOLD** squares together; press. Add a 2-1/2 x 4-1/2-inch **LIGHT GOLD** rectangle to the top edge of the unit; press. Sew an A unit to the top edge of the flower unit; press. Add a B unit to the left edge of the flower unit; press. *At this point the flower unit should measure 6-1/2-inches square.*

 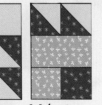

Make 1

Step 5 ✎ To make the stem unit, cut the 4-1/4-inch **BEIGE** square in half diagonally to make 2 triangles. Center a **BEIGE** triangle on the 1-1/2 x 7-inch **GREEN DIAGONAL CHECK** strip; stitch. Center the remaining **BEIGE** triangle on the opposite edge of the **GREEN DIAGONAL CHECK** strip; stitch and press. Trim the stem unit so it measures 4-1/2-inches square.

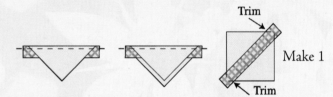

Trim

Make 1

Trim

Step 6 ✎ With right sides together, position a 1-1/2-inch **BEIGE** square on the right corner of the 1-1/2 x 6-1/2-inch **GREEN DIAGONAL CHECK** rectangle. Draw a diagonal line on the square; stitch, trim, and press. Repeat this process using a 1-1/2-inch **BEIGE** square and a 1-1/2 x 4-1/2-inch **GREEN DIAGONAL CHECK** rectangle. Notice the direction of the drawn line.

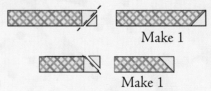

Make 1

Make 1

Step 7 ∾ With right sides together, position a 1-1/2 x 3-1/2-inch **BEIGE** rectangle on the right corner of a 1-1/2 x 4-1/2-inch **GREEN DIAGONAL CHECK** rectangle. Draw a diagonal line on the **BEIGE** rectangle; stitch, trim, and press. Repeat this process using a 1-1/2 x 3-1/2-inch **BEIGE** rectangle and a 1-1/2 x 2-1/2-inch **GREEN DIAGONAL CHECK** rectangle. Notice the direction of the drawn line.

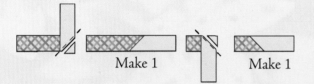

Make 1   Make 1

Step 8 ∾ Sew the stem and leaf units together; press. *At this point the unit should measure 6-1/2-inches square.*

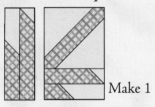

Make 1

Step 9 ∾ Sew the flower and stem/leaf units together in 2 vertical rows; press. Sew the rows together; press. *At this point the block should measure 12-1/2-inches square.*

A Quilter's Garden Block 10

A QUILTER'S GARDEN
BLOCK II - *Starburst*

CUTTING

From BEIGE PRINT:

❋ Cut 1, 4-1/4-inch square for stem unit

❋ Cut 1, 2-7/8 x 42-inch strip.
   From the strip cut:
   3, 2-7/8-inch squares
   4, 2-1/2 x 4-1/2-inch rectangles

From GOLD FLORAL:

❋ Cut 1, 4-1/2-inch square

❋ Cut 3, 2-1/2-inch squares

From MEDIUM GREEN PRINT:

❋ Cut 4, 2-1/2-inch squares

❋ Cut 1, 1-1/2 x 7-inch strip for stem unit

From DARK BLUE PRINT:

❋ Cut 1, 2-1/2 x 42-inch strip.
   From the strip cut:
   16, 2-1/2-inch squares
   3, 2-7/8-inch squares

From PINK PRINT:

❋ Cut 1, 2-1/2 x 42-inch strip.
   From the strip cut:
   4, 2-1/2 x 4-1/2-inch rectangles
   3, 2-1/2-inch squares

PIECING

Step 1 ✍ With right sides together, position a 2-1/2-inch **MEDIUM GREEN** square on the upper left corner and the lower right corner of a 4-1/2-inch **GOLD FLORAL** square. Draw a diagonal line on the **MEDIUM GREEN** squares; stitch, trim, and press. Repeat this process at the remaining corners of the **GOLD FLORAL** square. *At this point the unit should measure 4-1/2-inches square.*

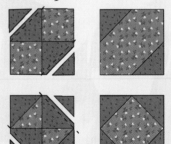

Make 1

Step 2 ✍ With right sides together, position a 2-1/2-inch **DARK BLUE** square on the corner of a 2-1/2 x 4-1/2-inch **PINK** rectangle. Draw a diagonal line on the square; stitch, trim, and press. Repeat this process at the opposite corner of the rectangle.

Make 4

Step 3 ✒ Repeat the Step 2 process with 2-1/2-inch **DARK BLUE** squares and the 2-1/2 x 4-1/2-inch **BEIGE** rectangles.

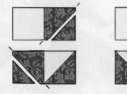 Make 4

Step 4 ✒ Sew the Step 3 units to the top edge of the Step 2 units; press. Referring to the block diagram, sew 2 of the units to the top and bottom edges of the Step 1 unit; press.

 Make 4

Step 5 ✒ With right sides together, layer the 2-7/8-inch **DARK BLUE** and **BEIGE** squares in pairs. Press together, but do not sew. Cut each square in half diagonally to make 6 sets of layered triangles. Stitch 1/4-inch from the diagonal edge of each pair of triangles; press. *At this point each triangle-pieced square should measure 2-1/2-inches square.*

Make 6, 2-1/2-inch
triangle-pieced squares

Step 6 ✒ Sew a 2-1/2-inch **GOLD FLORAL** square to the left edge of 3 of the triangle-pieced squares; press. Sew a 2-1/2-inch **PINK** square to the right edge of the remaining 3 triangle-pieced squares; press. Sew the 2 units together in pairs; press. *At this point each unit should measure 4-1/2-inches square.*

 Make 3

(continued on the next page)

Step 7 ✔ To make the stem unit, cut the 4-1/4-inch **BEIGE** square in half diagonally to make 2 triangles. Center a **BEIGE** triangle on the 1-1/2 x 7-inch **MEDIUM GREEN** strip; stitch. Center the remaining **BEIGE** triangle on the opposite edge of the **MEDIUM GREEN** strip; stitch and press. Trim the stem unit so it measures 4-1/2-inches square.

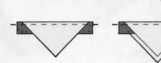
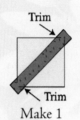

Make 1

Step 8 ✔ Sew the units together in 3 vertical rows; press. Sew the rows together; press. *At this point the block should measure 12-1/2-inches square.*

A QUILTER'S GARDEN Block 11

A Quilter's Garden
Block 12 - *Tulips*

Cutting

From BEIGE PRINT:
※ Cut 1, 2-7/8 x 42-inch strip.
   From the strip cut:
   5, 2-7/8-inch squares. Cut the
   squares in half diagonally to make
   10 triangles. You will use only 9.
   8, 2-1/2-inch squares
※ Cut 1, 2-1/2 x 42-inch strip.
   From the strip cut:
   7, 2-1/4-inch squares for stem unit

From LIGHT BLUE PRINT:
※ Cut 1, 2-7/8-inch square. Cut the
   square in half diagonally to make
   2 triangles.
※ Cut 2, 2-1/2 x 4-1/2-inch rectangles

From LIGHT GOLD PRINT:
※ Cut 1, 2-7/8-inch square. Cut the
   square in half diagonally to make
   2 triangles.
※ Cut 2, 2-1/2 x 4-1/2-inch rectangles

From PLUM PRINT #1:
※ Cut 1, 2-7/8-inch square. Cut the
   square in half diagonally to make
   2 triangles.
※ Cut 2, 2-1/2 x 4-1/2-inch rectangles

From LIGHT GREEN PRINT:
※ Cut 1, 2-7/8 x 42-inch strip.
   From the strip cut:
   5, 2-7/8-inch squares. Cut the
   squares in half diagonally to make
   10 triangles. You will use only 9.
   3, 2-1/2-inch squares
※ Cut 1, 1-1/2 x 42-inch strip.
   From the strip cut:
   7, 1-1/2 x 4-inch strips for stem unit

Piecing

Step 1 ✒ With right sides together,
position a 2-1/2-inch **BEIGE** square on
the right corner of a 2-1/2 x 4-1/2-inch
LIGHT BLUE rectangle. Draw a
diagonal line on the square; stitch, trim,
and press.

Make 1

Step 2 ✒ With right sides together,
position a 2-1/2-inch **LIGHT
GREEN** square on the right corner of
a 2-1/2 x 4-1/2-inch **LIGHT BLUE**
rectangle. Draw a diagonal line on the
square; stitch, trim, and press.

Make 1

 (continued on the next page)

BLOCK 12 - *Tulips* Continued

Step 3 ✎ With right sides together, position a 2-1/2-inch **BEIGE** square on the right corner of a 2-1/2 x 4-1/2-inch **LIGHT GOLD** rectangle. Draw a diagonal line on the square; stitch, trim, and press.

 Make 1

Step 4 ✎ With right sides together, position a 2-1/2-inch **LIGHT GREEN** square on the right corner of a 2-1/2 x 4-1/2-inch **LIGHT GOLD** rectangle. Draw a diagonal line on the square; stitch, trim, and press.

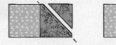 Make 1

Step 5 ✎ With right sides together, position a 2-1/2-inch **BEIGE** square on the right corner of a 2-1/2 x 4-1/2-inch **PLUM #1** rectangle. Draw a diagonal line on the square; stitch, trim, and press.

 Make 1

Step 6 ✎ With right sides together, position a 2-1/2-inch **LIGHT GREEN** square on the right corner of a 2-1/2 x 4-1/2-inch **PLUM #1** rectangle. Draw a diagonal line on the square; stitch, trim, and press.

 Make 1

Step 7 ✎ To make a stem unit, cut the 2-1/4-inch **BEIGE** squares in half diagonally to make 14 triangles. Center a **BEIGE** triangle on a 1-1/2 x 4-inch **LIGHT GREEN** strip; stitch. Center another **BEIGE** triangle on the opposite edge of the **LIGHT GREEN** strip; stitch and press. Trim the stem unit so it measures 2-1/2-inches square.

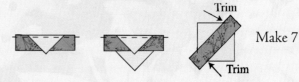 Make 7

Step 8 ✎ Sew together 6 of the **BEIGE** triangles and 6 of the **LIGHT GREEN** triangles in pairs and press to make 6, 2-1/2-inch triangle-pieced squares. Referring to the diagram, sew together in pairs, the triangle-pieced squares and 6 of the stem units; press. Sew the units together; press. *At this point each unit should measure 4-1/2-inches square.*

 Make 6 Make 3

Step 9 ✒ Sew together the remaining triangles in pairs; press. Sew a 2-1/2-inch **BEIGE** square to the top edge of each triangle-pieced square with the exception of the **PLUM/LIGHT GREEN** triangle-pieced square. Sew a stem unit to the top of this triangle-pieced square; press. *At this point each unit should measure 2-1/2 x 4-1/2-inches.*

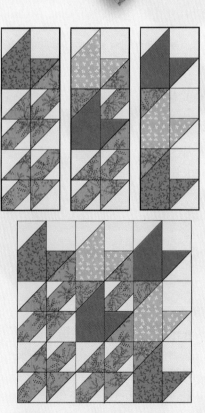

( )
Make 1 **LT. BLUE/BEIGE** unit

( )
Make 1 **LT. GOLD/BEIGE** unit

( )
Make 1 **PLUM/BEIGE** unit

( )
Make 1 **LT. BLUE/LT. GREEN** unit

(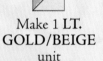)
Make 1 **LT. GOLD/LT. GREEN** unit

( )
Make 1 **PLUM/LT. GREEN** unit

Step 10 ✒ Refer to the block diagram to make the flower units. Sew the Step 9 units to the corresponding Step 1 through Step 6 units; press.

Step 11 ✒ Sew the units together in 3 vertical rows; press. Sew the rows together; press. *At this point the block should measure 12-1/2-inches square.*

A QUILTER'S GARDEN Block 12

FINISHING THE QUILT

QUILT CENTER

NOTE: *The side and corner triangles are larger than necessary and will be trimmed before the borders are added.*

CUTTING

From LIGHT GREEN FLORAL:
❊ Cut 2, 12-1/2 x 42-inch strips.
From the strips cut: 6, 12-1/2-inch alternate block squares.

From BEIGE FLORAL:
❊ Cut 2, 19 x 42-inch strips.
From the strips cut: 3, 19-inch squares, cutting each square twice diagonally to make 12 triangles. You will be using only 10 for side triangles. Also, cut 2, 10-inch squares, cutting each square once diagonally to make 4 corner triangles.

QUILT CENTER ASSEMBLY

Step 1 ❧ Referring to the quilt diagram, sew the pieced blocks, alternate blocks, and side triangles together in 6 diagonal rows. Press the seam allowances toward the alternate blocks and side triangles.

Step 2 ❧ Pin and sew the rows together; press. Add the corner triangles; press.

Step 3 ❧ Trim away excess fabric from the side and corner triangles, taking care to allow a 1/4-inch seam allowance beyond the corners of each block. See page 250 for complete instructions.

BORDERS

NOTE: *The yardage given allows for the border strips to be cut on the crosswise grain. Diagonally piece the strips as needed, referring to **Diagonal Piecing** diagrams under Step 1 on page 253. Read through **Border Basics** instructions on page 250, for general instructions on adding borders.*

CUTTING

From PLUM PRINT #2:
❊ Cut 8, 2-1/2 x 42-inch third middle border strips
❊ Cut 7, 1-1/2 x 42-inch inner border strips

From **LIGHT GREEN PRINT:**
❋ Cut 8, 2-1/2 x 42-inch first middle border strips

From **LARGE MULTICOLOR FLORAL:**
❋ Cut 10, 7-1/2 x 42-inch outer border strips
❋ Cut 8, 3-1/2 x 42-inch second middle border strips

ATTACHING THE BORDERS

Step 1 ✍ Attach the 1-1/2-inch wide **PLUM #2** inner border strips.

Step 2 ✍ Attach the 2-1/2-inch wide **LIGHT GREEN** first middle border strips.

Step 3 ✍ Attach the 3-1/2-inch wide **LARGE MULTICOLOR FLORAL** second middle border strips.

Step 4 ✍ Attach the 2-1/2-inch wide **PLUM #2** third middle border strips.

Step 5 ✍ Attach the 7-1/2-inch wide **LARGE MULTICOLOR FLORAL** outer border strips.

PUTTING IT ALL TOGETHER

❋ Cut the 7-1/8 yard length of backing fabric in half crosswise to make 3, 2-3/8 yard lengths. Refer to **Quilting the Project** on page 252 for complete instructions.

BINDING

From **MEDIUM GREEN PRINT:**
❋ Cut 10, 2-3/4 x 42-inch strips

Sew the binding to the quilt using a 3/8-inch seam allowance. This measurement will produce a 1/2-inch wide finished binding. Refer to **Binding** and **Diagonal Piecing** on page 253 for complete instructions.

PANSY PARK™

The classic elegance of
the traditional city park
graces your home
in this stunning quilt.

*T*he antique look and the traditional design of PANSY PARK make it
the most formal of the quilt designs in this book. The concept behind
PANSY PARK is of a city park with the medallion blocks in the middle of
the park – the flowers, trees and shrubs that are the park's essence -
being enclosed by the border of the quilt – perhaps a fence, a tree line or
hedge row. This is a very rich quilt with the gridwork of traditional
blocks being enhanced by the colors and piecing that all flow together.
PANSY PARK is truly an heirloom quilt—an important quilt—one that
you can pass on with pride. It is the type of quilt that, through the years,
has been made for special occasions like weddings and christenings.
When you quilt PANSY PARK,
you are making a quilt that will stand the test of time.

PANSY PARK

92 x 112 inches

Fabrics & Supplies

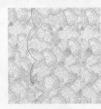

1-5/8 yards
BEIGE PRINT
for all 12 blocks

1/3 yard
GOLD/WINE PRINT
for blocks 1, 5, 6, 7, 8

1-1/8 yards **SMALL
GREEN LEAF PRINT**
for all 12 blocks

1/2 yard
RED FLORAL
for blocks 1, 4, 5, 11

1-1/8 yards
DARK GREEN PRINT
for blocks 1, 2, 4, 5, 7, 8, border

1/2 yard
GOLD PRINT
for blocks 2, 3, 10, 11

1-1/4 yards
RED PINE PRINT for
blocks 2, 3, 6, 7, 8, 9, 10, borders

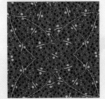

3/8 yard
MEDIUM BLUE PRINT
for blocks 3, 9, 10, 11

1-1/3 yards
GREEN STAR PRINT
for blocks 3, 6, 7

1/2 yard
LIGHT GOLD PRINT
for blocks 4, 7, 9, 12

3/4 yard
BEIGE LEAF PRINT
for middle border

1/2 yard
RED PRINT
for blocks 4, 5, 12, corner squares

7/8 yard
MULTICOLOR FLORAL
for middle border

1/4 yard
DARK BLUE PRINT
for blocks 6, 10, 12

7/8 yard
GREEN/GOLD FLORAL
for middle border

1/4 yard
LIGHT GREEN PRINT
for blocks 6, 8, 9, 11

1-3/8 yards
BEIGE DIAGONAL PRINT
for middle border

1-3/8 yards
TAN/ROSE FLORAL
for side and corner triangles

3 yards
LARGE GREEN LEAF PRINT
for outer border

1 yard
RED PINE PRINT
for binding

8 yards backing fabric
quilt batting,
at least 96 x 116-inches

Before beginning this project, read through **Getting Started** on page 244.

This fabric key should be used as a helpful guideline in selecting fabric for your quilt project. We cannot guarantee that a specific fabric will be available at your favorite quilt store, but suitable substitutions can be found.

Pansy Park

Block - *One*

Cutting

From BEIGE PRINT:

❋ Cut 1, 2-7/8 x 42-inch strip.
From the strip cut:
  2, 2-7/8-inch squares
  4, 2-1/2 x 4-1/2-inch rectangles
❋ Cut 1, 2-1/2 x 34-inch strip.
From the strip cut:
  8, 2-1/2-inch squares
  4, 1-1/2 x 2-1/2-inch rectangles

From GOLD/WINE PRINT:

❋ Cut 1, 2-1/2-inch square
❋ Cut 4, 1-1/2-inch squares

From SMALL GREEN LEAF PRINT:

❋ Cut 1, 2-1/2 x 42-inch strip.
From the strip cut:
  8, 2-1/2 x 4-1/2-inch rectangles

From RED FLORAL:

❋ Cut 2, 2-7/8-inch squares
❋ Cut 8, 2-1/2-inch squares

From DARK GREEN PRINT:

❋ Cut 2, 1-1/2 x 42-inch strips.
From the strips cut:
  2, 1-1/2 x 14-1/2-inch strips
  2, 1-1/2 x 12-1/2-inch strips

Piecing

Step 1 ✒ Sew a 1-1/2 x 2-1/2-inch **BEIGE** rectangle to the top and bottom edges of the 2-1/2-inch **GOLD/WINE PRINT** square; press. Sew 1-1/2-inch **GOLD/WINE PRINT** squares to the ends of the remaining 1-1/2 x 2-1/2-inch **BEIGE** rectangles; press. Sew these units to the side edges of the **GOLD/WINE PRINT** square; press.

Make 1

Step 2 ✒ With right sides together, position a 2-1/2-inch **RED FLORAL** square on the corner of a 2-1/2 x 4-1/2-inch **BEIGE** rectangle. Draw a diagonal line on the square and stitch on the line. Trim the seam allowance to 1/4-inch; press. Repeat this process at the opposite corner of the rectangle. *At this point each unit should measure 2-1/2 x 4-1/2-inches.*

Make 4

Step 3 ✒ Sew a 2-1/2 x 4-1/2-inch **SMALL GREEN LEAF PRINT** rectangle to the bottom edge of a Step 2 unit; press. Make 4 units. Sew a unit to both side edges of the Step 1 unit; press. The remaining units will be used in Step 6. *At this point the section should measure 4-1/2 x 12-1/2-inches.*

Make 4

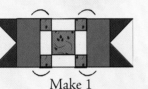

Make 1

Step 4 ✒ With right sides together, layer the 2-7/8-inch **BEIGE** and **RED FLORAL** squares. Press together, but do not sew. Cut the layered squares in half diagonally to make 4 sets of layered triangles. Stitch 1/4-inch from the diagonal edge of each pair of triangles; press. Sew a 2-1/2-inch **BEIGE** square to the left edge of each triangle-pieced square. *At this point each unit should measure 2-1/2 x 4-1/2-inches.*

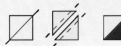

Make 4, 2-1/2-inch triangle-pieced squares

Make 4

Step 5 ✒ With right sides together, position a 2-1/2-inch **BEIGE** square on the corner of a 2-1/2 x 4-1/2-inch **SMALL GREEN LEAF PRINT** rectangle. Draw a diagonal line on the square; stitch, trim, and press. Make 4 units. Sew these units to the bottom edge of the Step 4 units; press. *At this point each unit should measure 4-1/2-inches square.*

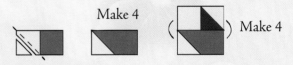

Make 4   Make 4

Step 6 ✒ Sew the Step 5 units to both side edges of the remaining Step 3 units; press. *At this point each section should measure 4-1/2 x 12-1/2-inches.*

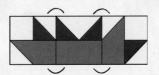

Make 2

(continued on the next page)

Step 7 ✒ Referring to the block diagram, sew the sections together; press. *At this point the block should measure 12-1/2-inches square.*

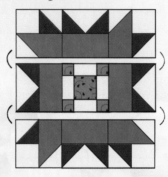

Step 8 ✒ Attach the 1-1/2-inch wide **DARK GREEN PRINT** border strips: press. *At this point the block should measure 14-1/2-inches square.*

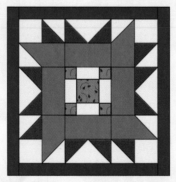

PANSY PARK Block 1

PANSY PARK
BLOCK - *Two*

CUTTING

From SMALL GREEN LEAF PRINT:
❋ Cut 1, 4-7/8 x 42-inch strip.
   From the strip cut:
      2, 4-7/8-inch squares
      1, 2-7/8 x 28-inch strip

From GOLD PRINT:
❋ Cut 2, 4-7/8-inch squares
❋ Cut 2, 2-1/2-inch squares

From RED PINE PRINT:
❋ Cut 6, 2-1/2-inch squares

From BEIGE PRINT:
❋ Cut 1, 2-7/8 x 28-inch strip

From DARK GREEN PRINT:
❋ Cut 2, 1-1/2 x 42-inch strips.
   From the strips cut:
      2, 1-1/2 x 14-1/2-inch strips
      2, 1-1/2 x 12-1/2-inch strips

PIECING

Step 1 ↝ With right sides together, layer the 4-7/8-inch **SMALL GREEN LEAF PRINT** and **GOLD** squares. Press together, but do not sew. Cut the layered squares in half diagonally to make 4 sets of layered triangles. Stitch 1/4-inch from the diagonal edge of each pair of triangles; press.

Make 4, 4-1/2-inch triangle-pieced squares

Step 2 ↝ With right sides together, position a 2-1/2-inch **GOLD** square on the **SMALL GREEN LEAF PRINT** corner of a Step 1 triangle-pieced square. Draw a diagonal line on the square; stitch, trim, and press. Make 2 units. Repeat this step positioning a 2-1/2-inch **RED PINE PRINT** square on the **SMALL GREEN LEAF PRINT** corner of a Step 1 triangle-pieced square; trim and press. Make 2 units. *At this point each unit should measure 4-1/2-inches square.* Sew the units together in pairs; press.

Make 2   Make 2

Make 2

(continued on the next page)

Step 3 ✐ With right sides together, layer the 2-7/8 x 28-inch **BEIGE** and **SMALL GREEN LEAF PRINT** strips, but do not sew. Cut the layered strips into squares. Cut the layered squares in half diagonally to make 16 sets of layered triangles. Stitch 1/4-inch from the diagonal edge of each pair of triangles; press.

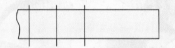

Crosscut 8, 2-7/8-inch squares

Make 16, 2-1/2-inch
triangle-pieced squares

Step 4 ✐ Sew the Step 3 triangle-pieced squares together in pairs; press. Sew 2 of these units to both side edges of the Step 2 units; press. *At this point each section should measure 4-1/2 x 12-1/2-inches.*

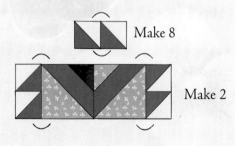

Make 8

Make 2

Step 5 ✐ Sew the remaining triangle-pieced square pairs together to make 2 strips; press. Sew 2-1/2-inch **RED PINE PRINT** squares to both ends of each strip; press. *At this point each section should measure 2-1/2 x 12-1/2-inches.*

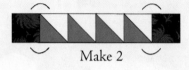

Make 2

Step 6 ✐ Referring to the block diagram, sew the sections together; press. *At this point the block should measure 12-1/2-inches square.*

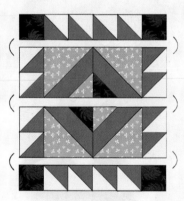

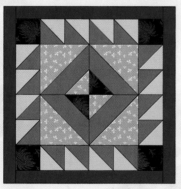

PANSY PARK Block 2

Step 7 ✎ Attach the
1-1/2-inch wide **DARK
GREEN PRINT** border
strips; press. *At this point
the block should measure
14-1/2-inches square.*

Pansy Park
Block - *Three*

Cutting

From GOLD PRINT:
❊ Cut 1, 2-1/2-inch square
❊ Cut 2, 1-1/2 x 42-inch strips.
  From the strips cut:
    8, 1-1/2 x 3-1/2-inch rectangles
    16, 1-1/2-inch squares

From MEDIUM BLUE PRINT:
❊ Cut 2, 1-1/2 x 4-1/2-inch rectangles
❊ Cut 2, 1-1/2 x 2-1/2-inch rectangles

From SMALL GREEN LEAF PRINT:
❊ Cut 2, 1-1/2 x 42-inch strips.
  From the strips cut:
    2, 1-1/2 x 6-1/2-inch rectangles
    2, 1-1/2 x 4-1/2-inch rectangles
    8, 1-1/2 x 3-1/2-inch rectangles
    4, 1-1/2-inch squares

From BEIGE PRINT:
❊ Cut 2, 1-1/2 x 42-inch strips.
  From the strips cut:
    4, 1-1/2 x 6-1/2-inch rectangles
    8, 1-1/2 x 2-1/2-inch rectangles
    20, 1-1/2-inch squares

From GREEN STAR PRINT:
❊ Cut 1, 2-1/2 x 42-inch strip.
  From the strip cut:
    4, 2-1/2-inch squares
    16, 1-1/2-inch squares

From RED PINE PRINT:
❊ Cut 2, 1-1/2 x 42-inch strips.
  From the strips cut:
    2, 1-1/2 x 14-1/2-inch strips
    2, 1-1/2 x 12-1/2-inch strips

PIECING

Step 1 ✍ Sew 1-1/2 x 2-1/2-inch **MEDIUM BLUE PRINT** rectangles to the top and bottom edges of the 2-1/2-inch **GOLD PRINT** square; press.

Step 2 ✍ With right sides together, position 1-1/2-inch **SMALL GREEN LEAF PRINT** squares on the corners of a 1-1/2 x 4-1/2-inch **MEDIUM BLUE PRINT** rectangle. Draw a diagonal line on the squares; stitch, trim, and press. *At this point each unit should measure 1-1/2 x 4-1/2-inches.* Make 2 units. Sew the units to both side edges of the Step 1 unit; press. *At this point the unit should measure 4-1/2-inches square.*

Make 2

Make 1

Step 3 ✍ Sew the 1-1/2 x 4-1/2-inch **SMALL GREEN LEAF PRINT** rectangles to the top and bottom edges of the Step 2 unit; press. Sew the 1-1/2 x 6-1/2-inch **SMALL GREEN LEAF PRINT** rectangles to the side edges of the unit; press.

Step 4 ✍ With right sides together, position 1-1/2-inch **GOLD** squares on the corners of a 1-1/2 x 3-1/2-inch **SMALL GREEN LEAF PRINT** rectangle. Draw a diagonal line on the squares; stitch, trim, and press. *At this point each unit should measure 1-1/2 x 3-1/2-inches.* Make 8 units. Repeat this process positioning 1-1/2-inch **BEIGE** squares on the corners of a 1-1/2 x 3-1/2-inch **GOLD** rectangle; stitch, trim, and press. Make 8 units. *At this point each unit should measure 1-1/2 x 3-1/2-inches.*

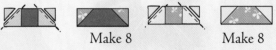
Make 8   Make 8

Step 5 ✍ Sew the Step 4 units together in pairs; press. Sew the pairs together; press. Sew a 1-1/2 x 6-1/2-inch **BEIGE** rectangle to the top edge of the units; press. *At this point each unit should measure 3-1/2 x 6-1/2-inches.*

Make 8

Make 4

211

(continued on the next page)

Step 6 ✏ Sew the Step 5 units to the side edges of the Step 3 unit; press. *At this point the section should measure 6-1/2 x 12-1/2-inches.*

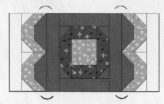

Step 7 ✏ With right sides together, position a 1-1/2-inch **GREEN STAR PRINT** square on the corner of a 1-1/2 x 2-1/2-inch **BEIGE** rectangle. Draw a diagonal line on the square; stitch, trim, and press. Repeat this process at the opposite corner of the rectangle. *At this point each unit should measure 1-1/2 x 2-1/2-inches.*

Make 8

Step 8 ✏ Sew a Step 7 unit to the top edge of a 2-1/2-inch **GREEN STAR PRINT** square; press. Make 4 units. Sew a 1-1/2-inch **BEIGE** square to each of the remaining Step 7 units; press. Sew a unit to the adjacent edge of the **GREEN STAR PRINT** square; press. Make 4 units. *At this point each unit should measure 3-1/2-inches square.* Sew the units to both side edges of the remaining Step 5 units; press.

At this point each section should measure 3-1/2 x 12-1/2-inches.

Make 4   Make 2

Step 9 ✏ Referring to the block diagram, sew the sections together; press. *At this point the block should measure 12-1/2-inches square.*

Step 10 ✏ Attach the 1-1/2-inch wide **RED PINE PRINT** border strips; press. *At this point the block should measure 14-1/2-inches square.*

PANSY PARK Block 3

PANSY PARK
BLOCK - *Four*

CUTTING

From RED FLORAL:
❋ Cut 2, 4-7/8-inch squares
❋ Cut 4, 2-1/2-inch squares

From LIGHT GOLD PRINT:
❋ Cut 2, 4-7/8-inch squares

From SMALL GREEN LEAF PRINT:
❋ Cut 1, 2-1/2 x 21-inch strip.
  From the strip cut:
    8, 2-1/2-inch squares

From RED PRINT:
❋ Cut 1, 2-1/2 x 20-inch strip.
  From the strip cut:
    4, 2-1/2 x 4-1/2-inch rectangles

From BEIGE PRINT:
❋ Cut 1, 2-1/2 x 42-inch strip.
  From the strip cut:
    8, 2-1/2 x 4-1/2-inch rectangles

From DARK GREEN PRINT:
❋ Cut 2, 1-1/2 x 42-inch strips.
  From the strips cut:
    2, 1-1/2 x 14-1/2-inch strips
    2, 1-1/2 x 12-1/2-inch strips

PIECING

Step 1 ✒ With right sides together, layer the 4-7/8-inch **RED FLORAL** and **LIGHT GOLD PRINT** squares. Press together, but do not sew. Cut the layered squares in half diagonally to make 4 sets of layered triangles. Stitch 1/4-inch from the diagonal edge of each pair of triangles; press.

 Make 4, 4-1/2-inch triangle-pieced squares

Step 2 ✒ With right sides together, position a 2-1/2-inch **SMALL GREEN LEAF PRINT** square on the **RED FLORAL** corner of a Step 1 triangle-pieced square. Draw a diagonal line on the square; stitch, trim, and press. Repeat this process on the **LIGHT GOLD** corner of the triangle-pieced square. *At this point each unit should measure 4-1/2-inches square.* Sew the units together in pairs; press. Sew the pairs together to make a square *which should measure 8-1/2-inches square.*

Make 4

Make 1

Step 3 ✒ With right sides together, position a 2-1/2 x 4-1/2-inch **BEIGE** rectangle on the corner of a 2-1/2 x 4-1/2-inch **RED PRINT** rectangle. Draw a diagonal line on the **BEIGE** rectangle; stitch, trim, and press. Repeat this process at the opposite corner of the **RED PRINT** rectangle. *At this point each unit should measure 2-1/2 x 8-1/2-inches.*

Make 4

Step 4 ✒ Sew Step 3 units to the side edges of the Step 2 square; press. *At this point the section should measure 8-1/2 x 12-1/2-inches.*

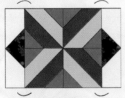

Step 5 ✒ Sew 2-1/2-inch **RED FLORAL** squares to both ends of the remaining Step 3 units; press. *At this point each section should measure 2-1/2 x 12-1/2-inches.*

Make 2

Step 6 ✒ Referring to the block diagram, sew the sections together; press. *At this point the block should measure 12-1/2-inches square.*

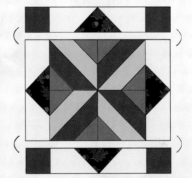

Step 7 ✒ Attach the 1-1/2-inch wide **DARK GREEN PRINT** border strips; press. *At this point the block should measure 14-1/2-inches square.*

PANSY PARK Block 4

215

Pansy Park
Block - *Five*

Cutting

From RED PRINT:
❋ Cut 1, 2-1/2-inch square
❋ Cut 1, 1-1/2 x 42-inch strip.
　From the strip cut:
　　20, 1-1/2-inch squares

From GOLD/WINE PRINT:
❋ Cut 4, 1-1/2 x 2-1/2-inch rectangles

From SMALL GREEN LEAF PRINT:
❋ Cut 12, 2-1/2-inch squares

From RED FLORAL:
❋ Cut 1, 2-1/2 x 42-inch strip.
　From the strip cut:
　　16, 2-1/2-inch squares

From BEIGE PRINT:
❋ Cut 2, 2-1/2 x 42-inch strips.
　From the strips cut:
　　8, 2-1/2 x 4-1/2-inch rectangles
　　4, 2-1/2-inch squares

From DARK GREEN PRINT:
❋ Cut 2, 1-1/2 x 42-inch strips.
　From the strips cut:
　　2, 1-1/2 x 14-1/2-inch strips
　　2, 1-1/2 x 12-1/2-inch strips

Piecing

Step 1 ✒ Sew a 1-1/2 x 2-1/2-inch **GOLD/WINE PRINT** rectangle to the top and bottom edges of the 2-1/2-inch **RED PRINT** square; press. Sew 1-1/2-inch **RED PRINT** squares to the ends of the remaining 1-1/2 x 2-1/2-inch **GOLD/WINE PRINT** rectangles; press. Sew these units to the side edges of the **RED PRINT** square; press.

Make 1

Step 2 ✒ With right sides together, position a 1-1/2-inch **RED PRINT** square on the upper left corner of a 2-1/2-inch **SMALL GREEN LEAF PRINT** square. Draw a diagonal line on the **RED PRINT** square; stitch, trim, and press. Repeat this process at the upper right corner of the **SMALL GREEN LEAF PRINT** square. *At this point each unit should measure 2-1/2-inches square. Make 8 units. Sew the units together in pairs; press. At this point each unit should measure 2-1/2 x 4-1/2-inches. (see diagram on next page)*

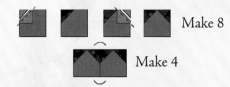 Make 8

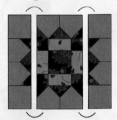 Make 4

Step 3 ✏ Sew Step 2 units to the top and bottom edges of the Step 1 unit; press. Sew 2-1/2-inch **SMALL GREEN LEAF PRINT** squares to the ends of the remaining Step 2 units; press. Sew these units to the sides of the Step 1 unit; press. *At this point the unit should measure 8-1/2-inches square.*

 Make 1

Step 4 ✏ With right sides together, position a 2-1/2-inch **RED FLORAL** square on the corner of a 2-1/2 x 4-1/2-inch **BEIGE** rectangle. Draw a diagonal line on the square; stitch, trim, and press. Repeat this process at the opposite corner of the rectangle. *At this point each unit should measure 2-1/2 x 4-1/2-inches.* Make a total of 8 units. Sew the units together in pairs; press. *At this point each unit should measure 2-1/2 x 8-1/2-inches.*

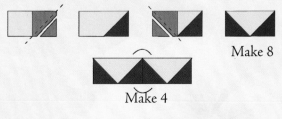 Make 8

Make 4

Step 5 ✏ Sew a Step 4 unit to both side edges of the Step 3 unit; press. *At this point the section should measure 8-1/2 x 12-1/2-inches.*

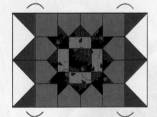 Make 1

Step 6 ✏ Sew 2-1/2-inch **BEIGE** squares to both side edges of the remaining Step 4 units; press. *At this point each section should measure 2-1/2 x 12-1/2-inches.*

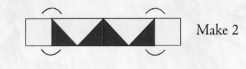 Make 2

(continued on the next page)

Step 7 ❧ Referring to the block diagram, sew the sections together; press. *At this point the block should measure 12-1/2-inches square.*

Step 8 ❧ Attach the 1-1/2-inch wide **DARK GREEN PRINT** border strips; press. *At this point the block should measure 14-1/2-inches square.*

PANSY PARK Block 5

Pansy Park
Block - *Six*

Cutting

From GOLD/WINE PRINT:
❊ Cut 1, 4-1/2-inch square

From SMALL GREEN LEAF PRINT:
❊ Cut 1, 2-1/2 x 42-inch strip.
  From the strip cut:
   2, 2-1/2 x 8-1/2-inch rectangles
   2, 2-1/2 x 4-1/2-inch rectangles
   4, 2-1/2-inch squares

From DARK BLUE PRINT:
❊ Cut 4, 2-1/2-inch squares

From GREEN STAR PRINT:
❊ Cut 8, 2-1/2-inch squares

From BEIGE PRINT:
❊ Cut 1, 2-1/2 x 42-inch strip.
  From the strip cut:
   4, 2-1/2 x 4-1/2-inch rectangles
   8, 2-1/2-inch squares

From LIGHT GREEN PRINT:
❊ Cut 4, 2-1/2-inch squares

From RED PINE PRINT:
❊ Cut 2, 1-1/2 x 42-inch strips.
  From the strips cut:
   2, 1-1/2 x 14-1/2-inch strips
   2, 1-1/2 x 12-1/2-inch strips

Piecing

Step 1 ✧ With right sides together, position a 2-1/2-inch **SMALL GREEN LEAF PRINT** square on the upper left corner of the 4-1/2-inch **GOLD/WINE PRINT** square. Draw a diagonal line on the **SMALL GREEN LEAF PRINT** square; stitch, trim, and press. Repeat this process at the lower right corner of the **GOLD/WINE PRINT** square. Repeat this process at the remaining 2 corners of the **GOLD/WINE PRINT** square. *At this point the unit should measure 4-1/2-inches square.*

Make 1

Step 2 ✧ With right sides together, position a 2-1/2-inch **DARK BLUE** square on both corners of a 2-1/2 x 8-1/2-inch **SMALL GREEN LEAF PRINT** rectangle. Draw a diagonal line on the squares; stitch, trim, and press. *At this point each unit should measure 2-1/2 x 8-1/2-inches.*

Make 2

(continued on the next page)

Step 3 ✂ Sew a 2-1/2 x 4-1/2-inch
SMALL GREEN LEAF PRINT
rectangle to the side edges of the
Step 1 unit; press. Sew the Step 2 units
to the top and bottom edges of the unit;
press. *At this point the unit should measure
8-1/2-inches square.*

Make 1

Step 4 ✂ With right sides together,
position a 2-1/2-inch **GREEN STAR
PRINT** square on the corner of a
2-1/2 x 4-1/2-inch **BEIGE** rectangle.
Draw a diagonal line on the square;
stitch, trim, and press. Repeat this
process at the opposite corner of the
rectangle. Sew 2-1/2-inch **BEIGE**
squares to both edges of these units;
press. *At this point each unit should measure
2-1/2 x 8-1/2-inches.*

Make 4   Make 4

Step 5 ✂ Sew 2 of the Step 4 units to
both side edges of the Step 3 unit;
press. *At this point the section should
measure 8-1/2 x 12-1/2-inches.*

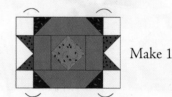

Make 1

Step 6 ✂ Sew a 2-1/2-inch **LIGHT
GREEN PRINT** square to both edges
of the remaining Step 4 units; press.
*At this point each section should measure
2-1/2 x 12-1/2-inches.*

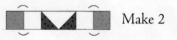

Make 2

Step 7 ✂ Referring to the block diagram,
sew the sections together; press. *At this
point the block should measure 12-1/2-inches
square.*

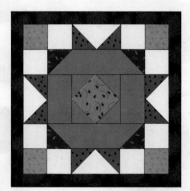

PANSY PARK Block 6

Step 8 🖋 Attach the
1-1/2-inch wide **RED
PINE PRINT** border
strips; press. *At this point
the block should measure
14-1/2-inches square.*

PANSY PARK

BLOCK - *Seven*

CUTTING

From RED PINE PRINT:
❋ Cut 1, 4-1/2-inch square
❋ Cut 4, 1-1/2 x 3-1/2-inch rectangles
❋ Cut 4, 1-1/2 x 2-1/2-inch rectangles

From BEIGE PRINT:
❋ Cut 1, 2-1/2 x 42-inch strip.
  From the strip cut:
    12, 2-1/2-inch squares
❋ Cut 1, 1-1/2 x 42-inch strip.
  From the strip cut:
    16, 1-1/2-inch squares

From SMALL GREEN LEAF PRINT:
❋ Cut 1, 2-1/2 x 42-inch strip.
  From the strip cut:
    8, 2-1/2 x 4-1/2-inch rectangles

From LIGHT GOLD PRINT:
❋ Cut 8, 2-1/2-inch squares

From GREEN STAR PRINT:
❋ Cut 1, 1-1/2 x 42-inch strip.
  From the strip cut:
    4, 1-1/2 x 4-1/2-inch rectangles
    4, 1-1/2 x 3-1/2-inch rectangles

From GOLD/WINE PRINT:
❋ Cut 4, 2-1/2-inch squares

From DARK GREEN PRINT:
❋ Cut 2, 1-1/2 x 42-inch strips.
  From the strips cut:
    2, 1-1/2 x 14-1/2-inch strips
    2, 1-1/2 x 12-1/2-inch strips

PIECING

Step 1 ✔ With right sides together, position a 2-1/2-inch **BEIGE** square on the upper left corner of a 4-1/2-inch **RED PINE PRINT** square. Draw a diagonal line on the **BEIGE** square; stitch, trim, and press. Repeat this process at the lower right corner of the **RED PINE PRINT** square. Repeat this process at the remaining 2 corners of the **RED PINE PRINT** square. *At this point the unit should measure 4-1/2-inches square.*

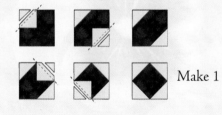

Make 1

Step 2 ✔ With right sides together, position a 2-1/2-inch **LIGHT GOLD PRINT** square on the corner of a 2-1/2 x 4-1/2-inch **SMALL GREEN LEAF PRINT** rectangle. Draw a diagonal line on the square; stitch, trim,

and press. Repeat this process at the opposite corner of the rectangle. *At this point each unit should measure 2-1/2 x 4-1/2-inches.*

Make 4

Step 3 ✎ With right sides together, position a 2-1/2-inch **BEIGE** square on the corner of a 2-1/2 x 4-1/2-inch **SMALL GREEN LEAF PRINT** rectangle. Draw a diagonal line on the square; stitch, trim, and press. Repeat this process at the opposite corner of the rectangle. *At this point each unit should measure 2-1/2 x 4-1/2-inches.* Sew a Step 2 unit to the bottom edge of each of these units; press. *At this point each unit should measure 4-1/2-inches square.*

Make 4   Make 4

Step 4 ✎ Sew a Step 3 unit to the side edges of the Step 1 unit; press. *At this point the section should measure 4-1/2 x 12-1/2-inches.*

Make 1

Step 5 ✎ With right sides together, position a 1-1/2-inch **BEIGE** square on the left corner of a 1-1/2 x 3-1/2-inch **RED PINE PRINT** rectangle. Draw a diagonal line on the square; stitch, trim, and press. Make 4 units. Repeat this process with a 1-1/2-inch **BEIGE** square and a 1-1/2 x 2-1/2-inch **RED PINE PRINT** rectangle. Notice the direction of the drawn line. Make 4 units.

Make 4   Make 4

Step 6 ✎ Sew the Step 5 units to the 2-1/2-inch **GOLD/WINE PRINT** squares; press.

Make 4

(continued on the next page)

Step 7 ✌ With right sides together, position a 1-1/2-inch **BEIGE** square on the left corner of a 1-1/2 x 4-1/2-inch **GREEN STAR PRINT** rectangle. Draw a diagonal line on the square; stitch, trim, and press. Make 4 units. Repeat this process with a 1-1/2-inch **BEIGE** square and a 1-1/2 x 3-1/2-inch **GREEN STAR PRINT** rectangle. Notice the direction of the drawn line. Make 4 units.

Make 4   Make 4

Step 8 ✌ Sew the Step 7 units to the Step 6 units; press. *At this point each unit should measure 4-1/2-inches square.*

Make 4

Step 9 ✌ Sew Step 8 units to the side edges of the remaining Step 3 units; press. *At this point each section should measure 4-1/2 x 12-1/2-inches.*

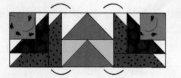

Make 2

Step 10 ✌ Referring to the block diagram, sew the sections together; press. *At this point the block should measure 12-1/2-inches square.*

Step 11 ✌ Attach the 1-1/2-inch wide **DARK GREEN PRINT** border strips; press. *At this point the block should measure 14-1/2-inches square.*

PANSY PARK Block 7

PANSY PARK
BLOCK - *Eight*

CUTTING

From SMALL GREEN LEAF PRINT:
* Cut 1, 2-1/2 x 42-inch strip.
   From the strip cut:
      4, 2-1/2 x 4-1/2-inch rectangles
      9, 2-1/2-inch squares

From RED PINE PRINT:
* Cut 1, 1-1/2 x 42-inch strip.
   From the strip cut:
      4, 1-1/2 x 2-1/2-inch rectangles
      20, 1-1/2-inch squares

From BEIGE PRINT:
* Cut 1, 2-1/2 x 42-inch strip.
   From the strip cut:
      4, 2-1/2 x 4-1/2-inch rectangles
      8, 1-1/2-inch squares
* Cut 1, 1-1/2 x 42-inch strip.
   From the strip cut:
      16, 1-1/2 x 2-1/2-inch rectangles

From GOLD/WINE PRINT:
* Cut 8, 2-1/2-inch squares

From LIGHT GREEN PRINT:
* Cut 4, 2-1/2-inch squares

From DARK GREEN PRINT:
* Cut 2, 1-1/2 x 42-inch strips.
   From the strips cut:
      2, 1-1/2 x 14-1/2-inch strips
      2, 1-1/2 x 12-1/2-inch strips

(continued on the next page)

PIECING

Step 1 ✎ With right sides together, position a 1-1/2-inch **BEIGE** square on the corner of a 1-1/2 x 2-1/2-inch **RED PINE PRINT** rectangle. Draw a diagonal line on the **BEIGE** square; stitch, trim, and press. Repeat this process at the opposite corner of the **RED PINE PRINT** rectangle.

 Make 4

Step 2 ✎ Sew a Step 1 unit to the top and bottom edges of a 2-1/2-inch **SMALL GREEN LEAF PRINT** square; press. Sew 1-1/2-inch **RED PINE PRINT** squares to the ends of the remaining Step 1 units; press. Sew these units to the side edges of the **SMALL GREEN LEAF PRINT** unit; press. *At this point each unit should measure 4-1/2-inches square.*

 Make 1

Step 3 ✎ With right sides together, position a 2-1/2-inch **GOLD/WINE PRINT** square on the corner of a 2-1/2 x 4-1/2-inch **SMALL GREEN LEAF PRINT** rectangle. Draw a diagonal line on the square; stitch, trim, and press. Repeat this process at the opposite corner of the rectangle.

 Make 4

Step 4 ✎ With right sides together, position a 2-1/2-inch **SMALL GREEN LEAF PRINT** square on the corner of a 2-1/2 x 4-1/2-inch **BEIGE** rectangle. Draw a diagonal line on the square; stitch, trim, and press. Repeat this process at the opposite corner of the rectangle. *At this point each unit should measure 2-1/2 x 4-1/2-inches.* Sew a Step 3 unit to the bottom edge of each of these units; press. *At this point each unit should measure 4-1/2-inches square.*

 Make 4

Step 5 ✎ Sew Step 4 units to both side edges of the Step 2 unit; press. *At this point the section should measure 4-1/2 x 12-1/2-inches.*

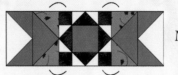 Make 1

Step 6 ✌ Sew a 1-1/2 x 2-1/2-inch **BEIGE** rectangle to the top and bottom edges of a 2-1/2-inch **LIGHT GREEN** square; press. Make 4 units. Sew 1-1/2-inch **RED PINE PRINT** squares to the ends of the remaining 1-1/2 x 2-1/2-inch **BEIGE** rectangles; press. Sew these units to the side edges of the **LIGHT GREEN** units; press.

Make 4

Step 7 ✌ Sew Step 6 units to both side edges of the remaining Step 4 units; press. *At this point each section should measure 4-1/2 x 12-1/2-inches.*

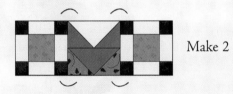
Make 2

Step 8 ✌ Referring to the block diagram, sew the sections together; press. *At this point the block should measure 12-1/2-inches square.*

Step 9 ✌ Attach the 1-1/2-inch wide **DARK GREEN PRINT** border strips; press. *At this point the block should measure 14-1/2-inches square.*

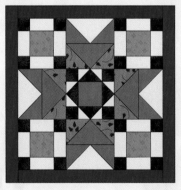

PANSY PARK Block 8

227

Pansy Park
Block - *Nine*

Cutting

From LIGHT GOLD PRINT:
❋ Cut 1, 3-1/2 x 42-inch strip.
   From the strip cut:
      8, 3-1/2-inch squares
      4, 1-1/2 x 2-1/2-inch rectangles

From MEDIUM BLUE PRINT:
❋ Cut 1, 2-1/2 x 42-inch strip.
   From the strip cut:
      4, 2-1/2-inch squares
      4, 1-1/2 x 2-1/2-inch rectangles
      12, 1-1/2-inch squares

From BEIGE PRINT:
❋ Cut 8, 1-1/2-inch squares

From RED PINE PRINT:
❋ Cut 1, 2-1/2-inch square
❋ Cut 4, 1-1/2 x 2-1/2-inch rectangles
❋ Cut 4, 1-1/2-inch squares

From SMALL GREEN LEAF PRINT:
❋ Cut 4, 3-1/2 x 6-1/2-inch rectangles

From LIGHT GREEN PRINT:
❋ Cut 1, 1-1/2 x 42-inch strip.
   From the strip cut:
      4, 1-1/2 x 3-1/2-inch rectangles
      4, 1-1/2 x 2-1/2-inch rectangles

Piecing

Step 1 ✐ With right sides together, position a 1-1/2-inch **MEDIUM BLUE** square on the corner of a 1-1/2 x 2-1/2-inch **LIGHT GOLD** rectangle. Draw a diagonal line on the square; stitch, trim, and press. Repeat this process at the opposite corner of the rectangle. *At this point each unit should measure 1-1/2 x 2-1/2-inches.*

 Make 4

Step 2 ✐ With right sides together, position a 1-1/2-inch **BEIGE** square on the corner of a 1-1/2 x 2-1/2-inch **MEDIUM BLUE** rectangle. Draw a diagonal line on the square; stitch, trim, and press. Repeat this process at the opposite corner of the rectangle. Sew these units to the top edge of the Step 1 units; press. *At this point each unit should measure 2-1/2-inches square.*

Make 4   Make 4

Step 3 ✎ Sew together the 1-1/2-inch **MEDIUM BLUE** and **RED PINE PRINT** squares in pairs; press. Sew a 1-1/2 x 2-1/2-inch **RED PINE PRINT** rectangle to the side edge of each of these units; press. *At this point the unit should measure 2-1/2-inches square.*

 Make 4

Step 4 ✎ Sew Step 2 units to the side edges of the 2-1/2-inch **RED PINE PRINT** square; press. Sew Step 3 units to both side edges of the remaining Step 2 units; press. Sew these units to the top and bottom edges of the **RED PINE PRINT** square unit; press. *At this point the unit should measure 6-1/2-inches square.*

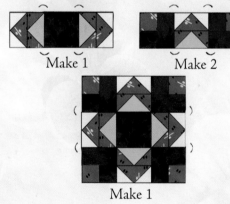

Make 1   Make 2

Make 1

Step 5 ✎ With right sides together, position a 3-1/2-inch **LIGHT GOLD PRINT** square on the corner of a 3-1/2 x 6-1/2-inch **SMALL GREEN LEAF PRINT** rectangle. Draw a

diagonal line on the square; stitch, trim, and press. Repeat this process at the opposite corner of the rectangle. *At this point each unit should measure 3-1/2 x 6-1/2-inches.*

Make 4

Step 6 ✎ Sew together the 1-1/2 x 2-1/2-inch **LIGHT GREEN** rectangles and the 2-1/2-inch **MEDIUM BLUE** squares in pairs; press. Sew a 1-1/2 x 3-1/2-inch **LIGHT GREEN** rectangle to the side edge of each of these units; press. *At this point each unit should measure 3-1/2-inches square.*

 Make 4

(continued on the next page)

Step 7 ✎ Sew Step 5 units to both side edges of the Step 4 unit; press. *At this point the section should measure 6-1/2 x 12-1/2-inches.*

Make 1

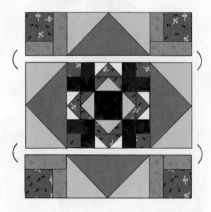

Step 8 ✎ Sew Step 6 units to both side edges of the remaining Step 5 units; press. *At this point each section should measure 3-1/2 x 12-1/2-inches.*

Make 2

Step 9 ✎ Referring to the block diagram, sew the sections together; press. *At this point the block should measure 12-1/2-inches square.*

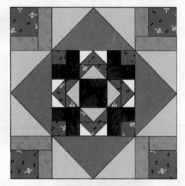

PANSY PARK Block 9

PANSY PARK
BLOCK - *Ten*

CUTTING

From MEDIUM BLUE PRINT:
❋ Cut 1, 3-1/4-inch square, cutting it twice diagonally to make 4 triangles

From SMALL GREEN LEAF PRINT:
❋ Cut 1, 3-1/2 x 42-inch strip.
 From the strip cut:
  4, 3-1/2 x 6-1/2-inch rectangles
  1, 2-1/2-inch square

From DARK BLUE PRINT:
❋ Cut 1, 1-1/2 x 42-inch strip.
 From the strip cut:
  20, 1-1/2-inch squares

From RED PINE PRINT:
❋ Cut 2, 3-1/4-inch squares, cutting each square twice diagonally to make 8 triangles

From BEIGE PRINT:
❋ Cut 1, 3-1/4 x 42-inch strip.
 From the strip cut:
  1, 3-1/4-inch square, cutting it twice diagonally to make 4 triangles
  4, 2-1/2-inch squares
  16, 1-1/2-inch squares

From GOLD PRINT:
❋ Cut 8, 3-1/2-inch squares

PIECING

Step 1 ✒ Layer a **MEDIUM BLUE** triangle on a **RED** triangle. Stitch along the bias edge as shown, being careful not to stretch the triangles. Press the seam allowance toward the **RED** triangle. Repeat to make 4 triangle units.

bias edges   Make 4

Step 2 ✒ Layer a **BEIGE** triangle on a **RED** triangle. Stitch along the bias edge as shown, being careful not to stretch the triangles. Press the seam allowance toward the **RED** triangle. Repeat to make 4 triangle units.

bias edges   Make 4

Step 3 ✒ Sew the Step 1 and Step 2 triangle units together in pairs; press. *At this point each hourglass unit should measure 2-1/2-inches square.*

Make 4

Step 4 ✒ Sew a 2-1/2-inch **BEIGE** square to both side edges of a Step 3 unit. Press the seam allowances toward the **BEIGE** squares. *At this point each unit should measure 2-1/2 x 6-1/2-inches.*

Make 2

(continued on the next page)

Step 5 ✔ Sew the remaining Step 3 units to both side edges of the 2-1/2-inch **SMALL GREEN LEAF PRINT** square. Press the seam allowances toward the **SMALL GREEN LEAF PRINT** square. *At this point the unit should measure 2-1/2 x 6-1/2-inches.*

 Make 1

Step 6 ✔ Sew the Step 4 units to the top and bottom edges of the Step 5 unit; press. *At this point the unit should measure 6-1/2-inches square.*

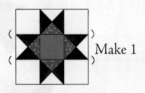 Make 1

Step 7 ✔ With right sides together, position a 3-1/2-inch **GOLD** square on the corner of a 3-1/2 x 6-1/2-inch **SMALL GREEN LEAF PRINT** rectangle. Draw a diagonal line on the square; stitch, trim, and press. Repeat this process at the opposite corner of the rectangle. *At this point each unit should measure 3-1/2 x 6-1/2-inches.*

 Make 4

Step 8 ✔ Sew Step 7 units to both side edges of the Step 6 unit; press. *At this point the section should measure 6-1/2 x 12-1/2-inches.*

 Make 1

Step 9 ✔ Sew 1-1/2-inch **DARK BLUE** squares to both sides of a 1-1/2-inch **BEIGE** square. Press the seam allowances toward the **DARK BLUE** squares. Sew 1-1/2-inch **BEIGE** squares to both sides of a 1-1/2-inch **DARK BLUE** square. Press the seam allowances toward the **DARK BLUE** squares. Sew the units together to make nine-patch units; press. *At this point each unit should measure 3-1/2-inches square.*

Make 8   Make 4   Make 4

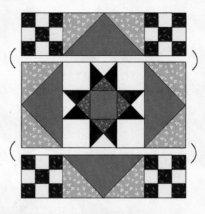

Step 10 ✒ Sew the Step 9 units to both side edges of the remaining Step 7 units; press. *At this point each section should measure 3-1/2 x 12-1/2-inches.*

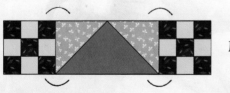

Make 2

Step 11 ✒ Referring to the block diagram, sew the Step 8 and Step 10 sections together; press. *At this point the block should measure 12-1/2-inches square.*

Pansy Park Block 10

PANSY PARK
BLOCK - *Eleven*

CUTTING

From MEDIUM BLUE PRINT:
✳ Cut 2, 2-7/8-inch squares
✳ Cut 8, 2-1/2-inch squares

From BEIGE PRINT:
✳ Cut 2, 2-7/8-inch squares
✳ Cut 8, 2-1/2-inch squares

From SMALL GREEN LEAF PRINT:
✳ Cut 1, 2-1/2 x 42-inch strip.
   From the strip cut:
      4, 2-1/2 x 4-1/2-inch rectangles
      4, 2-1/2-inch squares

From RED FLORAL:
✳ Cut 8, 2-1/2-inch squares

From GOLD PRINT:
✳ Cut 8, 2-1/2 x 4-1/2-inch rectangles

From LIGHT GREEN PRINT:
✳ Cut 4, 2-1/2-inch squares

PIECING

Step 1 ↝ With right sides together, layer the 2-7/8-inch **MEDIUM BLUE** and **BEIGE** squares. Press together, but do not sew. Cut the layered squares in half diagonally to make 4 sets of layered triangles. Stitch 1/4-inch from the diagonal edge of each pair of triangles; press. Sew the triangle-pieced squares together in pairs; press. Sew the pairs together; press. *At this point the pinwheel unit should measure 4-1/2-inches square.*

Make 4, 2-1/2-inch
triangle-pieced squares   Make 1

Step 2 ↝ With right sides together, position a 2-1/2-inch **BEIGE** square on the corner of a 2-1/2 x 4-1/2-inch **SMALL GREEN LEAF PRINT** rectangle. Draw a diagonal line on the square; stitch, trim, and press. Repeat this process at the opposite corner of the rectangle. *At this point each unit should measure 2-1/2 x 4-1/2-inches.*

 Make 4

Step 3 ✎ Sew Step 2 units to the top and bottom edges of the Step 1 unit; press. Sew 2-1/2-inch **SMALL GREEN LEAF PRINT** squares to both ends of the remaining Step 2 units; press. Sew these units to both side edges of the pinwheel unit; press. *At this point the unit should measure 8-1/2-inches square.*

Make 1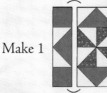

Step 4 ✎ With right sides together, position a 2-1/2-inch **MEDIUM BLUE** square on the left corner of a 2-1/2 x 4-1/2-inch **GOLD** rectangle. Draw a diagonal line on the square; stitch, trim, and press. Position a 2-1/2-inch **RED FLORAL** square on the right corner of the rectangle. Draw a diagonal line on the square; stitch, trim, and press. *At this point each unit should measure 2-1/2 x 4-1/2-inches.*

 Make 4

Step 5 ✎ With right sides together, position a 2-1/2-inch **RED FLORAL** square on the left corner of a 2-1/2 x 4-1/2-inch **GOLD** rectangle.

Draw a diagonal line on the square; stitch, trim, and press. Position a 2-1/2-inch **MEDIUM BLUE** square on the right corner of the rectangle. Draw a diagonal line on the square; stitch, trim, and press. Sew these units and the Step 4 units together in pairs; press. *At this point each unit should measure 2-1/2 x 8-1/2-inches.*

 Make 4

Make 4

Step 6 ✎ Sew Step 5 units to both side edges of the Step 3 unit; press. *At this point the section should measure 8-1/2 x 12-1/2-inches.*

 Make 1

(continued on the next page)

BLOCK - *Eleven* Continued

Step 7 ∽ Sew 2-1/2-inch **LIGHT GREEN** squares to both ends of the remaining Step 5 units; press. *At this point each section should measure 2-1/2 x 12-1/2-inches.*

 Make 2

Step 8 ∽ Referring to the block diagram, sew the sections together; press. *At this point the block should measure 12-1/2-inches square.*

PANSY PARK Block 11

PANSY PARK
BLOCK - *Twelve*

CUTTING

From DARK BLUE PRINT:
❋ Cut 5, 2-1/2-inch squares
❋ Cut 12, 1-1/2-inch squares

From SMALL GREEN LEAF PRINT:
❋ Cut 1, 1-1/2 x 42-inch strip.
   From the strip cut:
      2, 1-1/2 x 4-1/2-inch rectangles
      2, 1-1/2 x 2-1/2-inch rectangles
      4, 1-inch squares

From BEIGE PRINT:
❋ Cut 1, 1-1/2 x 42-inch strip.
   From the strip cut:
      16, 1-1/2-inch squares

From RED PRINT:
❋ Cut 8, 2-1/2-inch squares
❋ Cut 8, 1-1/2 x 2-1/2-inch rectangles

From LIGHT GOLD PRINT:
❋ Cut 1, 2-1/2 x 42-inch strip.
   From the strip cut:
      4, 2-1/2 x 4-1/2-inch rectangles
❋ Cut 2, 1-1/2 x 42-inch strips.
   From the strips cut:
      4, 1-1/2 x 10-1/2-inch rectangles
      8, 1-1/2 x 2-1/2-inch rectangles

PIECING

Step 1 ↝ With right sides together, position 1-inch **SMALL GREEN LEAF PRINT** squares on the corners of a 2-1/2-inch **DARK BLUE** square. Draw a diagonal line on the **SMALL GREEN LEAF PRINT** squares; stitch, trim, and press. *At this point the unit should measure 2-1/2-inches square.*

 Make 1

Step 2 ↝ With right sides together, position a 1-1/2-inch **DARK BLUE** square on both corners of a 1-1/2 x 4-1/2-inch **SMALL GREEN LEAF PRINT** rectangle. Draw a diagonal line on the squares; stitch, trim, and press. *At this point each unit should measure 1-1/2 x 4-1/2-inches.*

Make 2

(continued on the next page)

Step 3 ✒ Sew a 1-1/2 x 2-1/2-inch **SMALL GREEN LEAF PRINT** rectangle to both edges of the Step 1 unit; press. Sew the Step 2 units to the top and bottom edges of the unit; press. *At this point the unit should measure 4-1/2-inches square.*

Make 1

Step 4 ✒ With right sides together, position a 1-1/2-inch **BEIGE** square on the corner of a 1-1/2 x 2-1/2-inch **RED** rectangle. Draw a diagonal line on the square; stitch, trim, and press. Repeat this process at the opposite corner of the rectangle. Sew the units together in pairs; press. *At this point each unit should measure 1-1/2 x 4-1/2-inches.*

Make 8

Make 4

Step 5 ✒ Sew Step 4 units to both side edges of the Step 3 unit; press. *At this point the unit should measure 4-1/2 x 6-1/2-inches.*

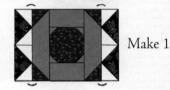

Make 1

Step 6 ✒ With right sides together, position a 2-1/2-inch **RED** square on the corner of a 2-1/2 x 4-1/2-inch **LIGHT GOLD** rectangle. Draw a diagonal line on the square; stitch, trim, and press. Repeat this process at the opposite corner of the rectangle. *At this point each unit should measure 2-1/2 x 4-1/2-inches.*

Make 4

Step 7 ✒ Sew Step 6 units to both side edges of the Step 5 unit; press. *At this point the section should measure 4-1/2 x 10-1/2-inches.*

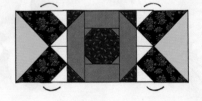

Make 1

Step 8 ✒ Sew the remaining Step 4 units and Step 6 units together in pairs; press.

Make 2

Step 9 ✒ Sew the 2-1/2-inch **DARK BLUE** squares and 1-1/2 x 2-1/2-inch **LIGHT GOLD** rectangles together in pairs; press. Sew the 1-1/2-inch **DARK BLUE** squares and the 1-1/2 x 2-1/2-inch **LIGHT GOLD** rectangles together in pairs; press. Sew the 2 units together in pairs; press. Sew these units to both side edges of the Step 8 units; press. *At this point each section should measure 3-1/2 x 10-1/2-inches.*

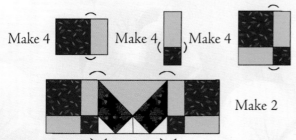
Make 4   Make 4   Make 4

Make 2

Step 10 ✒ Referring to the block diagram, sew the sections together; press. Sew 1-1/2 x 10-1/2-inch **LIGHT GOLD** rectangles to the top and bottom edges of the unit; press. Sew 1-1/2-inch **DARK BLUE** squares to both ends of the remaining

1-1/2 x 10-1/2-inch **LIGHT GOLD** rectangles; press. Sew the strips to both side edges of the block; press. *At this point the block should measure 12-1/2-inches square.*

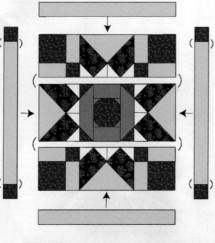

PANSY PARK Block 12

FINISHING THE QUILT

QUILT CENTER

Note: *The side and corner triangles are larger than necessary and will be trimmed before the borders are added.*

CUTTING

From TAN/ROSE FLORAL:
✻ Cut 2, 22 x 42-inch strips. From the strips cut: 2, 22-inch squares, cutting each square twice diagonally to make 8 triangles. You will be using only 6 for side triangles. Also, cut 2, 13-inch squares, cutting each square once diagonally to make 4 corner triangles.

QUILT CENTER ASSEMBLY

Step 1 ✒ Referring to the quilt diagram, sew the pieced blocks (Blocks 1 through 8) and side triangles together in 4 diagonal rows. Press the seam allowances in alternating directions by rows so the seams will fit snugly together with less bulk.

Step 2 ✒ Pin and sew the rows together; press. Add the corner triangles; press.

Step 3 ✒ Trim away excess fabric from the side and corner triangles, taking care to allow a 1/4-inch seam allowance beyond the corners of each block. Refer to **Trimming Side and Corner Triangles** on page 250 for complete instructions.

INNER BORDERS

Note: *To add borders with corner squares, refer to **Borders with Corner Squares** instructions on page 251. The yardage given allows for the border strips to be cut on the crosswise grain. Diagonally piece the strips as needed, referring to **Diagonal Piecing** instructions on page 253. Read through **Border** instructions on page 250 for general instructions on adding borders.*

CUTTING

From RED PINE PRINT:

❋ Cut 5, 1-1/2 x 42-inch border strips. Diagonally piece and cut:
2, 1-1/2 x 62-inch side border strips
2, 1-1/2 x 42-inch top/bottom border strips

From RED PRINT:

❋ Cut 4, 4-1/2-inch corner squares

From BEIGE LEAF PRINT:

❋ Cut 6, 3-1/2 x 42-inch border strips. Diagonally piece and cut:
2, 3-1/2 x 62-inch side border strips
2, 3-1/2 x 42-inch top/bottom border strips

From DARK GREEN PRINT:

❋ Cut 7, 1-1/2 x 42-inch border strips

ATTACHING THE INNER BORDERS

Step 1 ✒ Align long edges, sew together the top and bottom 1-1/2 x 42-inch RED PINE PRINT borders and the 3-1/2 x 42-inch BEIGE LEAF PRINT borders; press and trim. Sew the borders to the quilt; press.

Step 2 ✒ Aligning long edges, sew together the side 1-1/2 x 62-inch RED PINE PRINT borders and the 3-1/2 x 62-inch BEIGE LEAF PRINT borders; press and trim. Referring to **Borders with Corner Squares** on page 251, sew the 4-1/2-inch **RED PRINT** corner squares to both ends of the borders; press. Sew the borders to the quilt; press.

Step 3 ✒ Attach the 1-1/2-inch wide **DARK GREEN** borders; press.

Outer Borders

Cutting

Note: *The yardage given allows for the border strips to be cut on the crosswise grain. Diagonally piece the strips as needed, referring to* ***Diagonal Piecing*** *instructions on page 253. Read through* ***Border*** *instructions on page 250 for general instructions on adding borders. The* ***MULTICOLOR FLORAL, GREEN/GOLD PRINT****, and* ***BEIGE DIAGONAL PRINT*** *length measurements are generous and will need to be trimmed.*

From MULTICOLOR FLORAL:

❋ Cut 7, 3-1/2 x 42-inch border strips.
  Diagonally piece and cut:
  2, 3-1/2 x 72-inch side border strips
  2, 3-1/2 x 52-inch top/bottom border strips

From GREEN/GOLD PRINT:

❋ Cut 7, 3-1/2 x 42-inch border strips.
  Diagonally piece and cut:
  2, 3-1/2 x 72-inch side border strips
  2, 3-1/2 x 52-inch top/bottom border strips

From BEIGE DIAGONAL PRINT:

❋ Cut 7, 6-1/2 x 42-inch side border strips.
  Diagonally piece and cut:
  2, 6-1/2 x 72-inch side border strips
  2, 6-1/2 x 52-inch top/bottom border strips

From RED PINE PRINT:

❋ Cut 9, 1-1/2 x 42-inch border strips

From LARGE GREEN LEAF PRINT:

❋ Cut 12, 8-1/2 x 42-inch outer border strips

Attaching the Borders

Step 1 ✎ Aligning long edges, sew together the top and bottom 3-1/2 x 52-inch **MULTICOLOR FLORAL** borders, 3-1/2 x 52-inch **GREEN/GOLD** borders, and the 6-1/2 x 52-inch **BEIGE DIAGONAL PRINT** borders; press. Sew the borders to the quilt; press and trim.

Step 2 ✎ Aligning long edges, sew together the side 3-1/2 x 72-inch

MULTICOLOR FLORAL borders, 3-1/2 x 72-inch **GREEN/GOLD** borders, and the 6-1/2 x 72-inch **BEIGE DIAGONAL PRINT** borders; press and trim. Referring to **Borders with Corner Squares** instructions on page 251, sew blocks 9, 10, 11, and 12 to the ends of the borders; press. Sew the borders to the quilt; press.

Step 3 ✐ Attach the 1-1/2-inch wide **RED PINE PRINT** borders.

Step 3 ✐ Attach the 8-1/2-inch wide **LARGE GREEN LEAF PRINT** borders.

PUTTING IT ALL TOGETHER

Cut the 8 yard length of backing fabric in thirds crosswise to make 3, 2-2/3 yard lengths. Refer to **Quilting the Project** on page 252 for complete instructions.

BINDING

From RED PINE PRINT:
✳ Cut 11, 2-3/4 x 42-inch binding strips

Sew the binding to the quilt using a 3/8-inch seam allowance. This measurement will produce a 1/2-inch wide finished binding. Refer to **Binding and Diagonal Piecing** on page 253 for complete instructions.

GETTING STARTED

⌘

❋ Yardage is based on 42-inch wide fabric. If your fabric is wider or narrower it will affect the amount of necessary strips you need to cut in some patterns, and of course, it will affect the amount of fabric you have left over. Generally, THIMBLEBERRIES patterns allow for a little extra fabric so you can confidently cut your pattern pieces with ease.

❋ A rotary cutter, mat, and wide clear plastic ruler with 1/8-inch markings are needed tools in attaining accuracy. A beginner needs good tools just as an experienced quiltmaker needs good equipment. A 24 x 36-inch mat board is a good size to own. It will easily accommodate the average quilt fabrics and will aid in accurate cutting. The plastic ruler you purchase should be at least 6 x 24 inches and easy to read. Do not purchase a smaller ruler to save money; the large size will be invaluable to your quilt-making success.

❋ It is often recommended to prewash and press fabrics to test for color-fastness and possible shrinkage. If you choose to prewash, wash in cool water and dry in a cool to moderate dryer. Industry standards actually suggest that line drying is best. Shrinkage is generally very minimal and usually is not a concern. A good way to test your fabric for both shrinkage and color fastness is to cut a 3-inch square of fabric. Soak the fabric in a white bowl filled with water. Squeeze the water out of the fabric and press it dry on a piece of muslin. If the fabric is going to release color it will do so either in the water or when it is pressed dry. Re-measure the 3-inch fabric square to see if it has changed size considerably (more than 1/4 inch). If it has, wash, dry, and press the entire yardage. This little test could save you hours in prewashing and pressing.

❋ Read instructions thoroughly before beginning a project. Each step will make more sense to you when you have a general overview of the whole process. Take one step at a time and follow the illustrations. They will often make more sense to you than the words. Take "baby steps" so you don't get overwhelmed by the entire process.

✳ When working with flannel and other loosely woven fabrics, always prewash and dry. These fabrics almost always shrink some.

✳ For piecing, place right sides of the fabric pieces together and use 1/4-inch seam allowances throughout the entire quilt unless otherwise specifically stated in the directions. An accurate seam allowance is the most important part of the quilt-making process after accurate cutting. All the directions are based on accurate 1/4-inch seam allowances. It is very important to check your sewing machine to see in what position your fabric should be to get accurate seams. To test, use a piece of 1/4-inch graph paper, stitch along the quarter-inch line as if the paper were fabric. Make note of where the edge of the paper lines up with your presser foot or where it lines up on the throat plate of your machine. Many quilters place a piece of masking tape on the throat plate to help guide the edge of the fabric. Now test your seam allowance on fabric. Cut 2, 2-1/2-inch squares, place right sides together and stitch along one edge. Press seam allowances in one direction and measure. *At this point the unit should measure 2-1/2 x 4-1/2 inches.* If it does not, adjust your stitching guidelines and test again. Seam allowances are included in the cutting sizes given in this book.

✳ Pressing is the third most important step in quiltmaking. As a general rule, you should never cross a stitched seam with another seam unless it has been pressed. Therefore, every time you stitch a seam it needs to be pressed before adding another piece. Often, it will feel like you press as much as you sew, and often that is true. It is very important that you press and not iron the seams. Pressing is a firm, up-and-down motion that will flatten the seams but not distort the piecing. Ironing is a back-and-forth motion and will stretch and distort the small pieces. Most quilters use steam to help the pressing process. The moisture does help and will not distort the shapes as long as the pressing motion is used.

✳ An old-fashioned rule is to press seam allowances in one direction, toward the darker fabric. Often, background fabrics are light in color and pressing toward the darker fabric prevents the seam allowances from showing through to the right side. Pressing seam allowances in one direction is thought to create a stronger seam. Also, for ease in hand quilting, the quilting lines should fall on the side of the seam that is opposite the seam allowance. As you piece quilts, you will find these "rules" to be helpful but not necessarily always appropriate. Sometimes seams need to be pressed in the opposite direction so the seams of different units will fit together more easily, which quilters refer to as seams "nesting" together. When sewing together two units with opposing seam allowances, use the tip of your seam ripper to gently guide the units under your presser foot. Sometimes it is necessary to re-press the seams to make the units fit together nicely. Always try to achieve the least bulk in one spot and accept that no matter which way you press, it may be a little tricky and it could be a little bulky.

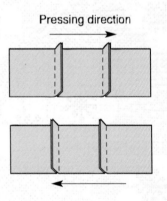

Pressing direction

SQUARING UP BLOCKS

To square up your blocks, first check the seam allowances. This is usually where the problem is, and it is always best to alter within the block rather than trim the outer edges. Next, make sure you have pressed accurately. Sometimes a block can become distorted by ironing instead of pressing.

To trim up block edges, use one of many clear plastic squares available on the market. Determine the center of the block; mark with a pin. Lay the square over the block and align as many perpendicular and horizontal lines as you can to the seams in your block. This will indicate where the block is off. Do not trim all off on one side; this usually results in real distortion of the pieces in the block and the block design. Take a little off all sides until the block is square. When assembling many blocks, it it necessary to make sure all are the same size.

TOOLS AND EQUIPMENT

Making beautiful quilts does not require a large number of specialized tools or expensive equipment. My list of favorites is short and sweet, and includes the things I use over and over again because they are always accurate and dependable.

❋ I find a long acrylic ruler indispensable for accurate rotary cutting. The ones I like most are an Omnigrid 6 x 24-inch grid acrylic ruler for cutting long strips and squaring up fabrics and quilt tops, and a Masterpiece 45, 8 x 24-inch ruler for cutting 6- to 8-inch wide borders. I sometimes tape together two 6 x 24-inch acrylic rulers for cutting borders up to 12 inches wide.

✳ A 15-inch Omnigrid square acrylic ruler is great for squaring up individual blocks and corners of a quilt top, for cutting strips up to 15 inches wide or long, and for trimming side and corner triangles.

✳ I think the markings on my 24 x 36-inch Olfa rotary cutting mat stay visible longer than on other mats, and the lines are fine and accurate.

✳ The largest size Olfa rotary cutter cuts through many layers of fabric easily, and it isn't cumbersome to use. The 2-1/2-inch blade slices through three layers of backing, batting, and a quilt top like butter.

✳ An 8-inch pair of Gingher shears is great for cutting out appliqué templates and cutting fabric from a bolt or fabric scraps.

✳ I keep a pair of 5-1/4-inch Gingher scissors by my sewing machine, so it is handy for both machine work and handwork. This size is versatile and sharp enough to make large and small cuts equally well.

✳ My Grabbit magnetic pincushion has a surface that is large enough to hold lots of straight pins, and a strong magnet that keeps them securely in place.

✳ Silk pins are long and thin, which means they won't leave large holes in your fabric. I like them because they increase accuracy in pinning pieces or blocks together, and it is easy to press over silk pins, as well.

✳ For pressing individual pieces, blocks, and quilt tops, I use an 18 x 48-inch sheet of plywood covered with several layers of cotton fiberfill and topped with a layer of muslin stapled to the back. The 48-inch length allows me to press an entire width of fabric at one time without the need to reposition it, and the square ends are better than tapered ends on an ironing board for pressing finished quilt tops.

ROTARY CUTTING

✳ Safety First! The blades of a rotary cutter are very sharp and need to be for accurate cutting. Look at a variety of cutters to find one that feels good in your hand. All quality cutters have a safety mechanism to "close" the cutting blade when not in use. After each cut and before laying the rotary cutter down, close the blade. Soon this will become second nature to you and will prevent dangerous accidents. Always keep cutters out of the sight of children. Rotary cutters are very tempting to fiddle with when they are lying around. When your blade is dull or nicked, change it. Damaged blades do not cut accurately and require extra effort that can also result in slipping and injury. Also, always cut away from yourself for safety.

❊ Fold the fabric in half lengthwise matching the selvage edges.

❊ "Square off" the ends of your fabric before measuring and cutting pieces. This means that the cut edge of the fabric must be exactly perpendicular to the folded edge, which creates a 90° angle. Align the folded and selvage edges of the fabric with the lines on the cutting board, and place a ruled square on the fold. Place a 6 x 24-inch ruler against the side of the square to get a 90° angle. Hold the ruler in place, remove the square, and cut along the edge of the ruler. If you are left-handed, work from the other end of the fabric. Use the lines on your cutting board to help line up fabric, but not to measure and cut strips. Use a ruler for accurate cutting, always checking to make sure your fabric is lined up with

horizontal and vertical lines on the ruler.

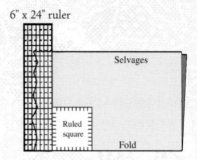

6" x 24" ruler

Selvages

Ruled square

Fold

CUTTING STRIPS

❊ When cutting strips or rectangles, cut on the crosswise grain. Strips can then be cut into squares or smaller rectangles.

❊ If your strips are not straight after cutting a few of them, refold the fabric, align the folded and selvage edges with the lines on the cutting board, and "square off" the edge again by trimming to straighten, and begin cutting.

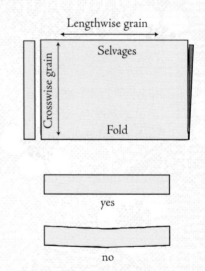

Lengthwise grain

Crosswise grain

Selvages

Fold

yes

no

SEWING LAYERED STRIPS TOGETHER

When you are instructed to layer strips, right sides together, and sew, you need to take some precautions. Gently lay a strip on top of another carefully lining up the raw edges. Pressing the strips together will hold them together nicely and a few pins here and there will also help. Be careful not to stretch the strips as you sew them together.

PRESSING STRIP SETS

❋ When sewing strips of fabric together for strip sets, it is important to press the seam allowances nice and flat, usually to the dark fabric. Be careful not to stretch as you press, causing a "rainbow effect." This will affect the accuracy and shape of the pieces cut from the strip set. Press on the wrong side first with the strips perpendicular to the ironing board. Flip the piece over and press on the right side to prevent little pleats from forming at the seams. Laying the strip set lengthwise on the ironing board seems to encourage the rainbow effect, as shown in diagram.

Avoid this
rainbow effect

CUTTING SIDE AND CORNER TRIANGLES

In projects with side and corner triangles, the instructions have you cut side and corner triangles larger than needed. This will allow you to square up the quilt and eliminates the frustration of ending up with precut side and corner triangles that don't match the size of your pieced blocks.

To cut triangles, first cut squares. The project directions will tell you what size to make the squares and whether to cut them in half to make two triangles or to cut them in quarters to make four triangles, as shown in the diagrams. This cutting method will give you side triangles that have the straight of grain on the outside edges of the quilt. This is a very important part of quiltmaking that will help stabilize your quilt center.

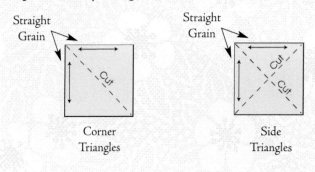

Straight Grain — Cut

Corner Triangles

Straight Grain — Cut

Side Triangles

TRIMMING SIDE AND CORNER TRIANGLES

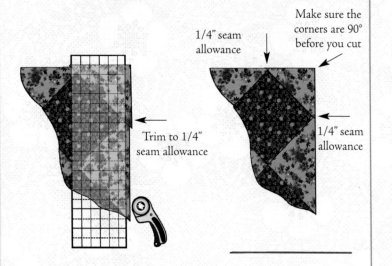

1/4" seam allowance

Trim to 1/4" seam allowance

Make sure the corners are 90° before you cut

1/4" seam allowance

❋ Begin at a corner by lining up your ruler 1/4 inch beyond the points of the corners of the blocks as shown.

❋ Cut along the edge of the ruler. Repeat this procedure on all four sides of the quilt top.

BORDER BASICS

❋ Note: Cut borders to the width called for. Always cut border strips a few inches longer than needed, just to be safe. Diagonally piece the border strips together as needed.

Step 1 ✍ With pins, mark the center points along all four sides of the quilt. For the top and bottom borders, measure the quilt from left to right through the middle.

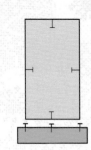

Step 2 ✍ Measure and mark the border lengths and center points on the strips cut for the borders before sewing them on.

Step 3 ✍ Pin the border strips to the quilt and stitch a 1/4-inch seam. Press the seam allowances toward the borders. Trim off excess border lengths.

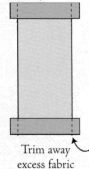

Trim away excess fabric

Step 4 ✍ For the side borders, measure your quilt from top to bottom, including the borders just added, to determine the length of the side borders.

Step 5 ✍ Measure and mark the side border lengths as you did for the top and bottom borders.

Step 6 ✍ Pin and stitch the side border strips in place. Press and trim the border strips even with the borders just added.

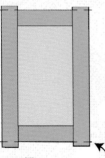

Trim away excess fabric

Step 7 ✒ If your quilt has multiple borders, measure, mark, and sew additional borders to the quilt in the same manner.

Borders with Corner Squares

Step 1 ✒ Measure, mark, and sew the top and bottom borders to the quilt. Trim away the excess fabric.

Step 2 ✒ For the side borders, measure just the quilt top including seam allowances, but not the top and bottom borders. Cut the side borders to this length. Sew a corner square to each end of these border strips. Sew the borders to the quilt; press.

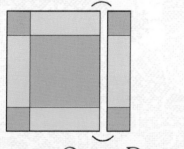

Choosing a Quilt Design

Quilting is such an individual process that it is difficult to recommend designs for each quilt. There are hundreds of quilting stencils available at quilt shops. (Templates are used generally for appliqué shapes; stencils are used for marking quilting designs.)

There are a few suggestion that may help you decide how to quilt your project, depending on how much time you would like to spend quilting. Many quilters now use professional long arm quilting machines or hire someone skilled at running these machines to do the quilting. This, of course, frees up more time to piece.

Quilting Suggestions

❋ Repeat one of the design elements in the quilt as part of the quilting design.

❋ Two or three parallel rows of echo quilting outside an appliqué piece will highlight the shape.

❋ Stipple or meander quilting behind a feather or central motif will make the primary design more prominent.

❋ Look for quilting designs that will cover two or more borders, rather than choosing separate designs for each individual border.

❋ Quilting in the ditch of seams is an effective way to get a project quilted without a great deal of time marking the quilt.

Marking the Quilting Design

❋ When marking the quilt top, use a marking tool that will be visible on the quilt fabric and yet will be easy enough to remove. Always test your marking tool on a scrap of fabric before marking the entire quilt.

Along with a multitude of commercial marking tools available, you may find that very thin slivers of hand soap (Dial, Ivory, etc.) work really well for marking medium- to dark-color fabrics. The thin lines of soap show up nicely and they are easily removed by simply rubbing gently with a piece of like-colored fabric.

Basting

❋ Mark the quilt top for quilting. Layer the backing, batting and quilt top. To secure the layers together for hand quilting, use long basting stitches by hand to hold the layers together. Quilt as desired.

Quilting the Project

❋ Now that your quilt is finished it needs to be layered with batting and backing, and prepared for quilting. Whether it is machine quilted or hand quilted, it is best to baste all 3 layers together. You may hand baste with large basting stitches or pin baste with medium size brass safety pins. Many quilters are satisfied with spray adhesives which are available at local quilt shops.

Step 1 ✌ Press the completed quilt top on the back side first, carefully clipping and removing hanging threads. Then press the quilt front making sure all seams are flat and all loose threads are removed.

Step 2 ✌ Remove the selvages from the backing fabric. Sew the long edges together; press. Trim the backing and batting so they are 4 inches larger than the quilt top.

Step 3 ✌ Mark the quilt top for quilting. Layer the backing, batting, and quilt top. Baste the 3 layers together and quilt. Work from the center of the quilt out to the edges. This will help keep the quilt flat by working the excess of the 3 layers to the outside edges.

Step 4 ✎ When quilting is complete, remove basting. Hand baste the 3 layers together a scant 1/4 inch from the edge. This basting keeps the layers from shifting and prevents puckers from forming when adding the binding. Trim excess batting and backing fabric even with the edge of the quilt top.

BINDING BASICS

❋ The instructions for each quilt indicate the width to cut the binding used in that project. The measurements are sufficient for a quilt made of cotton quilting fabrics and medium low loft quilt batting. If you use a high loft batt or combine a fluffy high loft batt with flannel fabrics, you may want to increase the width of the binding strips by adding 1/4 to 1/2 inch to the cut width of your binding. Always test a small segment of the binding before cutting all the strips needed.

Step 1 ✎ Diagonally piece the binding strips. Fold the strip in half lengthwise, wrong sides together, and press.

Stitch diagonally   Trim to 1/4" seam allowance   Press seam open

Step 2 ✎ Unfold and trim one end at a 45° angle. Turn under the edge 1/4 inch and press. Refold the strip.

Fold Line

Step 3 ✎ With raw edges of the binding and quilt top even, stitch with a 3/8-inch seam allowance starting 2 inches from the angled end. Miter the binding at the corners. As you approach a corner of the quilt, stop sewing 3/8 inch from the corner of the quilt.

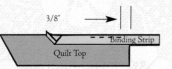

3/8"   Binding Strip   Quilt Top

Step 4 ✎ Clip the threads and remove the quilt from under the presser foot. Flip the binding strip up and away from the quilt, then fold the binding down even with the raw edge of the quilt. Begin sewing at the upper edge. Miter all 4 corners in this manner.

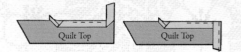

Quilt Top   Quilt Top

Step 5 ✎ Trim the end of the binding so it can be tucked inside of the beginning binding about 3/8 inch. Finish stitching the seam.

Step 6 ❧ Turn the folded edge of the binding over the raw edges and to the back of the quilt so that the stitching line does not show. Hand sew the binding in place, folding in the mitered corners as you stitch.

Quilt Back   Quilt Back   Quilt Back

Rod Casing or Sleeve to Hang Quilts

To hang wall quilts, attach a casing that is made of the same fabric as the quilt back. Attach this casing at the top of the quilt, just below the binding. Often, it is helpful to attach a second casing at the bottom of the quilt so you can insert a dowel into it which will help weight the quilt and make it hang free of ripples.

To make a rod casing or "sleeve," cut enough strips of fabric equal to the width of the quilt plus 2 inches for side hems. Generally, 6-inch wide strips will accommodate most rods. If you are using a rod with a larger diameter, increase the width of the strips.

Seam the strips together to get the length needed; press. Fold the strip in half lengthwise, wrong sides together. Stitch the long raw edges together with a

1/4-inch seam allowance. Center the seam on the back side of the sleeve; press. The raw edges of the seam will be concealed when the sleeve is stitched to the back of the quilt. Turn under both of the short raw edges; press and stitch to hem the ends. The final measurement should be about 1/2 inch from the quilt edges.

Pin the sleeve to the back of the quilt so the top edge of the sleeve is just below the binding. Hand stitch the top edge of the sleeve in place, then the bottom edge. Make sure to knot and secure your stitches at each end of the sleeve to make sure it will not pull away from the quilt with use. Slip the rod into the casing. If your wall quilt is not directional, making a sleeve for the bottom edge will allow you to turn your quilt end to end to relieve the stress at the top edge. You could also slip a dowel into the bottom sleeve to help anchor the lower edge of the wall quilt.

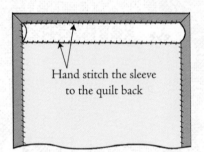

Hand stitch the sleeve to the quilt back

QUILT BACKING BASICS

Yardage Requirements and Piecing Suggestions

Crib
45 x 60"

2-3/4 yards
Cut 2, 1-3/8-yard lengths

Twin
72 x 90"

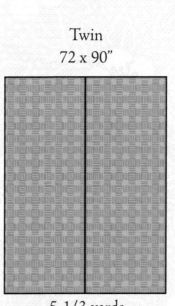

5-1/3 yards
Cut 2, 2-2/3-yard lengths

Double/Full
81 x 96"

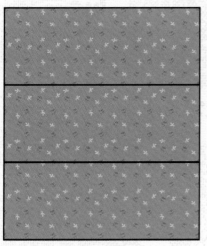

7-1/8 yards
Cut 3, 2-3/8-yard lengths

Queen
90 x 108"

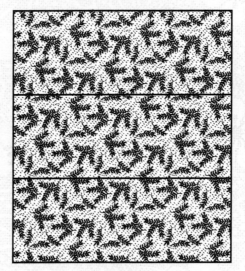

8 yards
Cut 3, 2-5/8-yard lengths

FROM THE PUBLISHER

⌘

THIMBLEBERRIES Design Studio was started by Lynette Jensen more than 16 years ago. Based in Hutchinson, Minnesota, THIMBLEBERRIES grew out of Lynette's love for antique quilts and the rich, family traditions they represented.

Lynette's ability to combine color, pattern and texture with clear, straightforward instructions has created legions of devotees worldwide. Her books and patterns have sold over a million copies, helping to create successful quilters around the globe. Today, there are more than 850 THIMBLEBERRIES Quilt Clubs devoted to Lynette's designs.

THIMBLEBERRIES *Big Book of Quilt Blocks* offers you, your family and friends the opportunity to enjoy this singular approach to quilting. Enjoy.

James L. Knapp
President—Publishing Solutions, LLC